The Mysterious Universe written by: Robin Kerrod
Illustrated by: Max Ansell, Gordon Davies, Philip Ems,
          John Harwood, Len Huxter, Lee Noel, John Marshall

Our Planet Earth written by: Keith Lye
Illustrated by: Max Ansell, Gordon Davies, Roger Full Associates,
          Angela Heaseman, Duncan Mill, Pat Mynot, Lee Noel,
          Geoff Taylor.

Designed by: Tri-Art
Series Editor: Christopher Tunney
Art Director: Keith Groom

**Published by Christensen Press Limited, The Grange,
Grange Yard, London SE1 3AG.**
© Christensen Press Limited 1985

First published 1985
Revised edition 1990

Printed and bound by Graficas Reunidas, Madrid, Spain.

ISBN: 0 946994 00 5

The Mysterious Universe

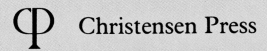

Christensen Press

THE NIGHT SKY   The night sky has a beauty we can all enjoy. The stars sparkle like jewels on a velvet background. The Moon, always changing its shape, pours its silvery light into the darkness. At first sight, the night sky appears to be filled haphazardly with stars. But, after a while, we find that we can recognize patterns of stars and thus find our way through the heavens. By studying the heavens, we become astronomers. Astronomy is perhaps the oldest science of all. The Chaldeans and the Babylonians were skilled observers of the heavens over 5,000 years ago.

What are the constellations?

Constellations are the patterns the bright stars make in the sky. Ancient astronomers imagined they could see the shapes of animals, people, and other things in the pattern of the stars, and named the constellations accordingly. In astronomy the constellations are known by their Latin names, such as *Leo* (the Lion).

Pisces, the Fishes

Leo, the Lion

Scorpio, the Scorpion

Ursa Major, the Great Bear

Orion, the Hunter

Why do they move?

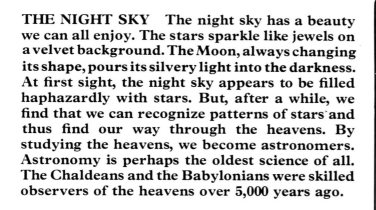

If you remain stargazing for long enough, you notice that the constellations move through the heavens hour by hour. In 24 hours they are more or less back where they started. This happens because the Earth is spinning in space, once every 24 hours. Ancient astronomers thought that the stars were fixed on the inside of a great celestial sphere that circled around the Earth.

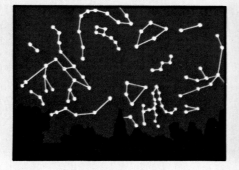

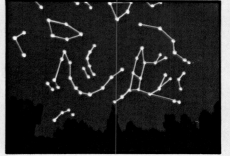

Can we ever see all the constellations?

Which constellations you can see depends on where you are on Earth. The best place to be is near the Equator. There you can, over the year, see almost all the constellations. If you live elsewhere, there are some constellations you will never see.

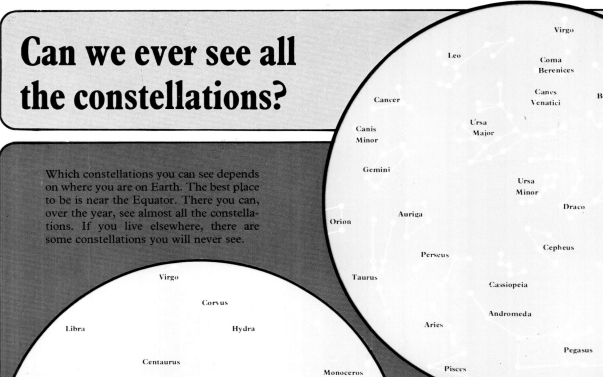

Constellations of the Northern Hemisphere

Constellations of the Southern Hemisphere

The Zodiac

Throughout the year, the Sun, the Moon, and the planets appear to travel through a narrow band of the heavens. It is called the *zodiac*. There are 12 constellations along this band, called the *signs of the zodiac*. The positions of the heavenly bodies in the zodiac are thought by some people to influence our lives and future actions. This belief is the basis of astrology. Astrologers were very important people in ancient times.

What is the pole star?

The pole star is a star almost directly above the Earth's North Pole. This means that as the Earth spins, the pole star appears to stay in the same place. When you take a long-exposure photograph of the northern sky, the pole star appears as a dot. The other stars show up as arcs.

How big is the Moon?

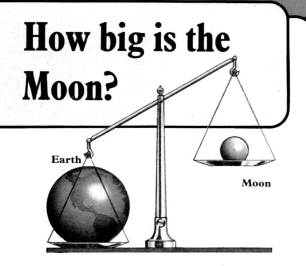

Earth

Moon

The Moon is very much smaller than the Earth. Its diameter is only about a quarter that of the Earth. If the Earth were hollow, you could fit nearly 50 Moons into it. Because it is small, the Moon has a small gravity. If you went to the Moon, you could jump six times higher than you can on Earth.

THE SILVER MOON The Earth and the Moon travel through space together. The Moon is the Earth's satellite. It circles around the Earth about once a month. Our word "month" comes from "moon." We know more about the Moon than about any other body in outer space. This is because men from Earth have actually landed on the Moon and explored its surface. They have brought back lunar soil and rocks. ("Lunar" means "of the Moon.") The Moon is by far the Earth's nearest neighbor in space. It lies only about 240,000 miles (385,000 km) away. This is just a stone's throw in space. The other heavenly bodies lie many millions of miles away.

What is the Moon's surface like?

The Moon is so close that we can see many details of its surface from Earth. The bright regions are rugged highlands covered with holes, or *craters*. The dark regions are flat, and are called *maria* (seas).

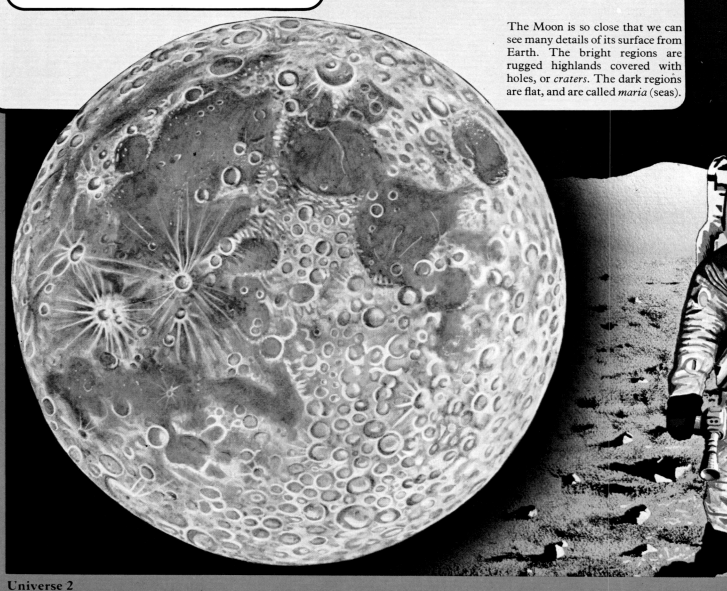

Why can we see only one side?

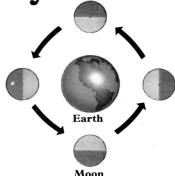

If you study the Moon from month to month, you notice that it keeps the same face toward us all the time. The reason is that the Moon spins on its own axis while it is traveling around the Earth. Every time it circles the Earth once, it spins once on its axis.

Why does the Moon change shape?

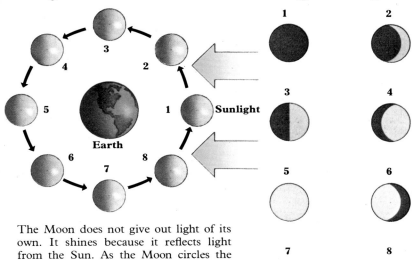

The Moon does not give out light of its own. It shines because it reflects light from the Sun. As the Moon circles the Earth, the Sun lights up different parts of it. From Earth it looks as if the Moon is changing shape. We call these changing shapes the Moon's *phases*.

Moon's phases

What is it like on the Moon?

The Apollo astronauts who visited the Moon found that it is a lifeless, barren wasteland. There is no air on the Moon, nor any water. It is scorching hot by day, and very cold at night. The surface is covered with dust, and there are rocks strewn around everywhere between the many craters.

THE SOLAR SYSTEM The Earth and the Moon belong to a family of bodies that travels through space with the Sun. We call this family the solar system. The most important members of the family are the nine bodies we call the planets. The Earth is a planet. In order of increasing distance from the Sun the other planets are: Mercury, Venus, (Earth), Mars, Jupiter, Saturn, Uranus, Neptune, and Pluto.

Who thought of a solar system?

In the third century, BC, a Greek astronomer called Aristarchus first suggested that the Earth revolved around the Sun, and not the other way around. But no one else believed this until a Polish priest, Nicolaus Copernicus (above), introduced the idea again in 1543.

How do the planets move?

The planets move in two different ways in space. One, they spin on their axes like tops. Two, they travel around the Sun in great oval paths, or *orbits*. Viewed from the north, they move counterclockwise.

How big are they?

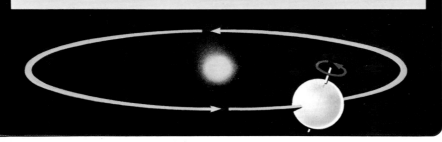

Mercury   Venus   Earth   Mars

Jupiter

The biggest planets by far are Jupiter and Saturn, which have diameters of 88,600 and 74,700 miles respectively (142,600 and 120,200 km). If Jupiter were hollow, it could swallow over 1,300 Earths; Saturn could swallow over 750. Uranus and Neptune are near twins, with diameters of about 31,000 miles (50,000 km). Next in size, but very much smaller, comes the Earth, followed by its neighbors Venus and Mars. The smallest of the planets is believed to be the one closest to the Sun—Mercury, with a diameter of only 3,015 miles (4,850 km). The outermost planet, Pluto, is also small, and may in fact be smaller than Mercury.

How far from Earth are the other planets?

None of the planets comes very near the Earth. Even the nearest, Venus, never gets closer than about 26 million miles (42 million km). This is over 100 times farther away than the Moon. The farthest planet, Pluto, never comes much closer than about 3,000 million miles (5,000 million km).

Pluto

Neptune

Uranus

Saturn

What else circles the Sun?

Many other bodies circle the Sun besides the planets. They include the *satellites*, or moons, which circle around the planets. There are also the shapeless lumps of rock that we call the *asteroids* or minor planets. There are even smaller bodies still, which we see in the night sky as *comets* and *meteors*.

Asteroid

THE LIFE-GIVING SUN (1) The Sun is our star. It is very much like millions of other stars in the sky. It appears bigger and brighter only because it is so very much closer to us. It lies 93 million miles (150 million km) away. It has a diameter of 865,000 miles (1,400,000 km)— about 115 times that of the Earth.

What is the Sun made of?

Like all ordinary stars, the Sun is a massive ball of white-hot gas. Most of it is hydrogen gas. If you could cut into the Sun, you would find that it would get hotter and hotter the deeper you went. The outer surface has a temperature of about 10,000°F (6,000°C). But in the center, the temperature is as high as 27,000,000°F. (15,000,000°C). We call the visible surface of the Sun the *photosphere* ("light-sphere").

How does the Sun affect us?

The Sun affects everything on Earth in one way or another. It gives the Earth heat, light, and life. Plants need the energy in sunlight to make food, and we all rely on plant life to live. Fuels exist thanks to the Sun, since they are plant remains. The Sun causes our weather, because it heats the air, the land, and the oceans.

Why does the Sun turn red at sunset?

When the Sun is low in the evening sky, it often appears blood-red. This happens because of dust in the atmosphere. The dusty atmosphere acts as a kind of filter, which lets through mainly red light. A red night often means that the following day will be clear.

The Sun is all-important to life on Earth, and practically all ancient peoples worshipped it as a god. The ancient Egyptians named their Sun-god *Ra*. The Greeks and Romans named him *Apollo*. The Aztecs of Mexico, the Incas of Peru, and the Mayas of Central America were also Sun worshippers.

Why does the Sun shine?

The Sun is like a huge atomic furnace. It "burns" atoms of hydrogen in its very hot center. The atoms fuse, or combine, to form atoms of helium. When this happens, great amounts of energy are given out as light and heat. Humans have imitated this process in the terrifying hydrogen bomb.

Will the Sun always shine?

The Sun will continue to shine as it does now for another 5,000 million years. Then it will swell into a red giant star so large that it will extend beyond the Earth's orbit. It will then shrink into a white dwarf star little bigger than the Earth.

What is the Sun's surface like?

The surface is a sea of white-hot gas. Here and there, tongues of flaming gas, or *flares*, shoot upward. Sometimes, great fountains of gas erupt and are hundreds of thousands of miles high. We call them *prominences*. On some parts of the surface, there are dark regions that we call *sunspots*. They are cooler than the rest of the surface.

What is an eclipse?

An eclipse is what happens when one heavenly body moves into the shadow cast in space by another. An eclipse of the Sun occurs when the Moon moves in between the Sun and the Earth. It casts a tiny shadow on the Earth.

An eclipse of the Moon occurs when the Moon moves into the shadow cast in space by the Earth. Because the Earth is quite large compared with the Moon, it casts a big shadow. The Moon can spend up to $2\frac{1}{2}$ hours in this shadow.

What is a total eclipse?

A total eclipse occurs when the Moon's disk exactly covers the disk of the Sun. At the beginning of an eclipse, the Moon starts to cover the bright Sun. Daylight fades into twilight. At the moment of total eclipse, day suddenly turns into night for up to 7 minutes. Then the sky brightens as the Sun reappears.

Ancient peoples used to fear eclipses. The Chinese thought a huge dragon was trying to swallow the Sun. They made a great noise to frighten it away. It always worked!

How did the Sun form?

The Sun was born from a great cloud of gas and dust. In time, the cloud started to spin, and became a disk with a bulge at the center. Gradually, the bulge got smaller and hotter, and eventually began to shine as the Sun. The gas and dust in the disk came together to form the planets.

PLANET EARTH Ancient peoples thought that the Earth was the center of the universe. But we now know that it is a mere planet—one of nine that circle the Sun in space. Among the planets, the Earth is quite small. Its diameter is only 7,926 miles (12,756 km) at the Equator. This is less than one-tenth the diameter of Jupiter. The Earth lies about 93 million miles (150 million km) from the Sun, and makes one journey around the Sun in $365\frac{1}{4}$ days (1 year). It spins around on its axis once every 24 hours (1 day).

What is special about the Earth?

Though it may be small, the Earth is without doubt one of the most beautiful bodies in space, as pictures taken from space show. Also it is unique among the planets in several respects. Most important, it supports life in thousands upon thousands of different forms—from tiny creatures too small for the eye to see, to giant trees and such huge animals as the elephant and whale. It is a watery planet. The water helps to support life and shape the surface. The Earth itself is alive. Its crust still ripples and splits with earthquakes. Volcanoes still erupt, disgorging molten rock from the Earth's interior.

What causes the seasons?

March 21
**Spring in
N. Hemisphere**

**Autumn in
S. Hemisphere**

December 21

June 21
**Summer in
N. Hemisphere**

**Winter in
S. Hemisphere**

Sun

September 21

**Autumn in
N. Hemisphere**

**Spring in
S. Hemisphere**

**Winter in
N. Hemisphere
Summer in
S. Hemisphere**

The regular changes in climate we call the *seasons* occur because the Earth's axis is tilted in relation to its path around the Sun. Places receive more or less heat according to whether they are tilted more towards or away from the Sun.

Why is the atmosphere so important?

The atmosphere is the thin layer of gases that surrounds the Earth. Though it is thin, it is very important. It gives us oxygen to breathe. Without oxygen, there could be little life on Earth. The atmosphere acts as a blanket to keep us warm at night when the Sun goes in. It filters out rays from the Sun that could burn us, and protects us from rocks from space.

What are the Northern and Southern lights?

In far northern and far-southern regions of the world, nature puts on a splendid fireworks display. The night sky is lit up with flames and moving curtains of colored light. Such a display is called the *Northern Lights* in the north and the *Southern Lights* in the south. Its proper name is *aurora*. Aurorae are caused by particles from outer space hitting the atmosphere.

Can we see other planets with the naked eye?

You can see three of the planets very easily—Venus, Jupiter, and Mars. They shine like very bright stars. But unlike the stars, they wander across the celestial sphere month by month. The word *planet* means *wanderer*. You can also see Mercury and Saturn if you know where to look. But Uranus, Neptune, and Pluto are too faint to be seen.

THE PLANETS (1) The planets are the biggest members of the Sun's family, but compared with the Sun they are tiny. The Sun has 750 times more mass than all the planets put together! The planets are very different in appearance and make-up. That is what makes them so fascinating. Some of the other eight planets are smaller than the Earth. Others are bigger. None of them is much like the Earth. Those closer to the Sun become very much hotter than the Earth ever does. And those farther away get very much colder. They are not places where people from Earth could live.

October 1977

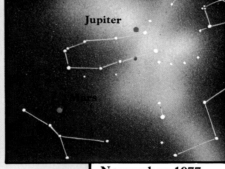

November 1977

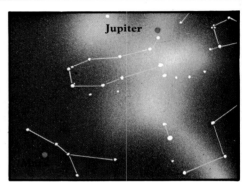

December 1977

Why do they shine?

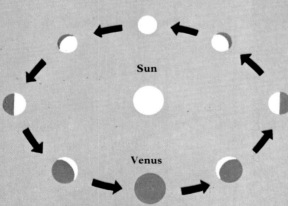

Phases of Venus as seen from Earth

The planets do not shine because they have their own light, as the Sun does. They shine because they reflect the Sun's light, just as the Moon does. And like the Moon, the planets appear to change shape, when viewed from the Earth. This is because we can see different amounts of the sunlit surface as the planet moves through the heavens.

What are the planets made of?

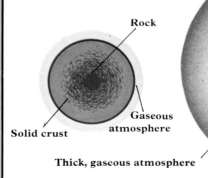

Rock

Solid crust

Gaseous atmosphere

Thick, gaseous atmosphere

Rocky core

Solid gas

Liquid gas

There is a great difference in make-up between the small planets and the giant ones. The small ones—Mercury, Venus, Earth, Mars, and Pluto—are made of rock. They have little, if any, atmosphere around them. The giant planets, Jupiter, Saturn, Uranus, and Neptune, are made up almost entirely of gas. This gas may exist as a liquid, or even a solid near the center of the planet.

Do they all have moons?

The Earth is not alone among the planets in having a moon, or *satellite*, circling around it. Pluto has one moon, Mars two, while the giant planets are like miniature solar systems with a large number of satellites circling them: Jupiter has 16, Saturn 21, Uranus 15 and Neptune 8. Some of these moons are bigger than Earth's Moon.

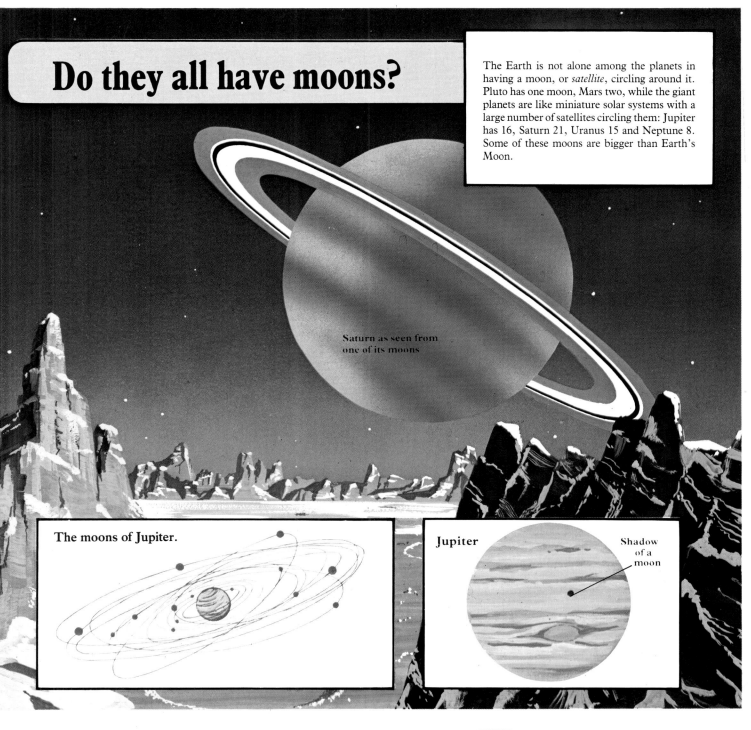

Saturn as seen from one of its moons

The moons of Jupiter.

Jupiter

Shadow of a moon

Do other suns have planets?

The Sun is only one of thousands of millions of stars in the heavens. It would be very odd if it were the only one to have planets circling around it. Astronomers reckon that planetary systems are quite common. So there should be other planets like the Earth somewhere. But they would be too far away for us to see.

THE PLANETS (2)

What is the evening star?

The planet Venus is the evening star. At certain times of the year it appears in the western sky as a bright star, just after sunset. At other times, it becomes the morning star, for it appears in the eastern sky just before sunrise. Venus is a very hot planet covered by thick clouds of carbon dioxide gas.

Mars is the red planet. It shines in the night sky with a distinct reddish light. This is because its surface is red. Photographs taken by space probes have shown its color. Mars has a slight atmosphere of carbon dioxide. Its surface is barren and marked with craters and volcanoes. There does not appear to be any life.

Which is the red planet?

Which is the giant planet?

Jupiter is the giant planet. If it were the size of a football, then the Earth would be only the size of a marble. Through a telescope, Jupiter shows a disk crossed with parallel dark and light bands. These are thought to be the tops of clouds in its thick hydrogen atmosphere. They form bands because the planet is spinning around very fast.

What is the red spot?

The red spot is a huge oval mark often visible in the southern part of Jupiter's disk. It is thought to be caused by a gigantic storm that has been raging on the planet for many centuries. Other spots and marks appear on Jupiter from time to time, but they are not so distinctive.

Which is the ringed planet?

Saturn is known as the ringed planet because a set of flat rings surrounds it at the equator. Only two of the four rings are bright. We can see them at different angles, year by year. They are probably made of ice and dust, and are very thin. They almost disappear from view when we look at them edge-on.

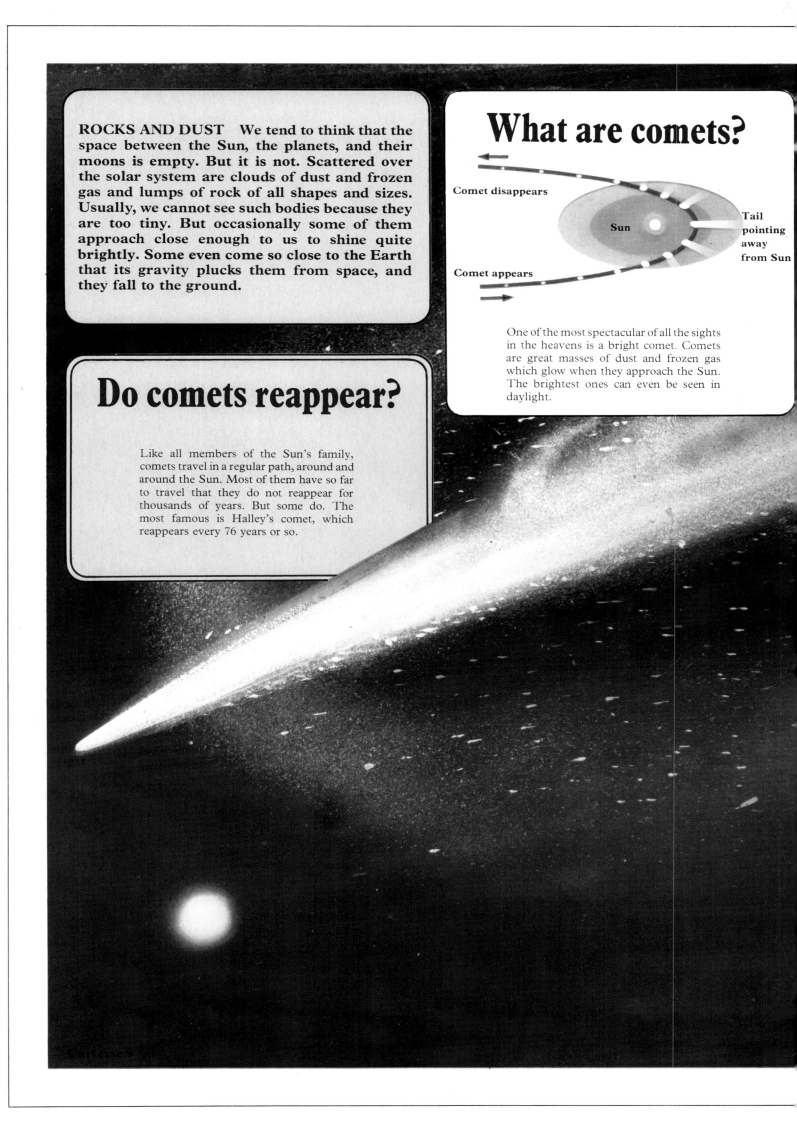

ROCKS AND DUST We tend to think that the space between the Sun, the planets, and their moons is empty. But it is not. Scattered over the solar system are clouds of dust and frozen gas and lumps of rock of all shapes and sizes. Usually, we cannot see such bodies because they are too tiny. But occasionally some of them approach close enough to us to shine quite brightly. Some even come so close to the Earth that its gravity plucks them from space, and they fall to the ground.

What are comets?

Comet disappears

Comet appears

Sun

Tail pointing away from Sun

One of the most spectacular of all the sights in the heavens is a bright comet. Comets are great masses of dust and frozen gas which glow when they approach the Sun. The brightest ones can even be seen in daylight.

Do comets reappear?

Like all members of the Sun's family, comets travel in a regular path, around and around the Sun. Most of them have so far to travel that they do not reappear for thousands of years. But some do. The most famous is Halley's comet, which reappears every 76 years or so.

Bayeux Tapestry

The comet we know as *Halley's comet* has been seen many times over the years. It reappeared, for example, in 1066, at about the time of the Battle of Hastings. It is shown on the Bayeux tapestry, which commemorates William the Conqueror's victory over the English.

What are asteroids?

The asteroids are the largest of the rocky lumps in the solar system. They circle in a broad belt between the planets Mars and Jupiter. The biggest, called *Ceres*, is about 470 miles (750 km) across.

What are meteors?

When bits of rock are captured by the Earth, they plunge through the upper air. There, they are heated up by friction and start to burn. From the ground, this shows up as a fiery streak, which we call a *meteor*.

What are meteorites?

Most of the bits of rock that cause meteors burn up into dust. But some are big enough to reach the ground. We call them *meteorites*. Some are made up mainly of iron and nickel, not rock.

Where is the largest crater?

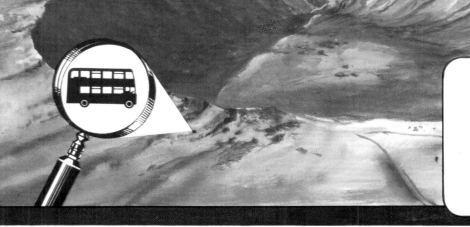

If a meteorite is very large, it makes a huge hole, or crater, when it hits the ground. A few craters can still be found on Earth. The biggest, in Arizona, measures 4,150 feet (1,265 meters) across, and is 575 feet (175 meters) deep in places. Most Moon craters were caused by the impact of meteorites.

How far away are the stars?

Our star, the Sun, lies 93 million miles (150 million km) away. The next nearest star lies over 25 million million miles (40 million million km) away. It is called *Proxima Centauri*. Its light takes some $4\frac{1}{3}$ years to travel to the Earth. We say it lies $4\frac{1}{3}$ light-years away.

THE DISTANT STARS Gazing at the stars is endlessly interesting. Even with the naked eye, we can see that they are not all alike. Most of them are white. Others are tinged yellow, red, orange, blue or green. Some stars seem much brighter than others. This is because they lie at different distances from us, and the farther away they are, the fainter they appear. Many of the stars are only about as bright as the Sun. But some are tens of thousands of times brighter.

What are they made of?

Like the Sun, a star is made up mostly of hydrogen gas. This gas fuels the star's nuclear furnace, which produces its heat and light. Stars also contain traces of some of the other chemical elements found on Earth, including iron.

Why do stars twinkle?

On most nights when you look at the stars, you notice that they seem to twinkle. But the twinkling has nothing to do with the stars. It happens because layers of air at different temperatures bend starlight this way and that as it passes through the atmosphere.

How many stars are there?

If you were very patient, you might be able to count about 5,000 stars in the sky with the naked eye. Through binoculars or a telescope, you would see many thousands more. Altogether astronomers estimate there are at least 100,000 million in the star system our Sun belongs to.

Do the stars shine steadily?

Ignoring twinkling, most stars shine steadily year in, year out. But some vary in brightness regularly. They are called *variable stars*. Stars called *novae* (new stars) suddenly flare up and then fade again. Others, called *supernovae*, flare up so violently they blast themselves apart.

Surface of supergiant

How big are they?

White dwarf

Sun

Giant star

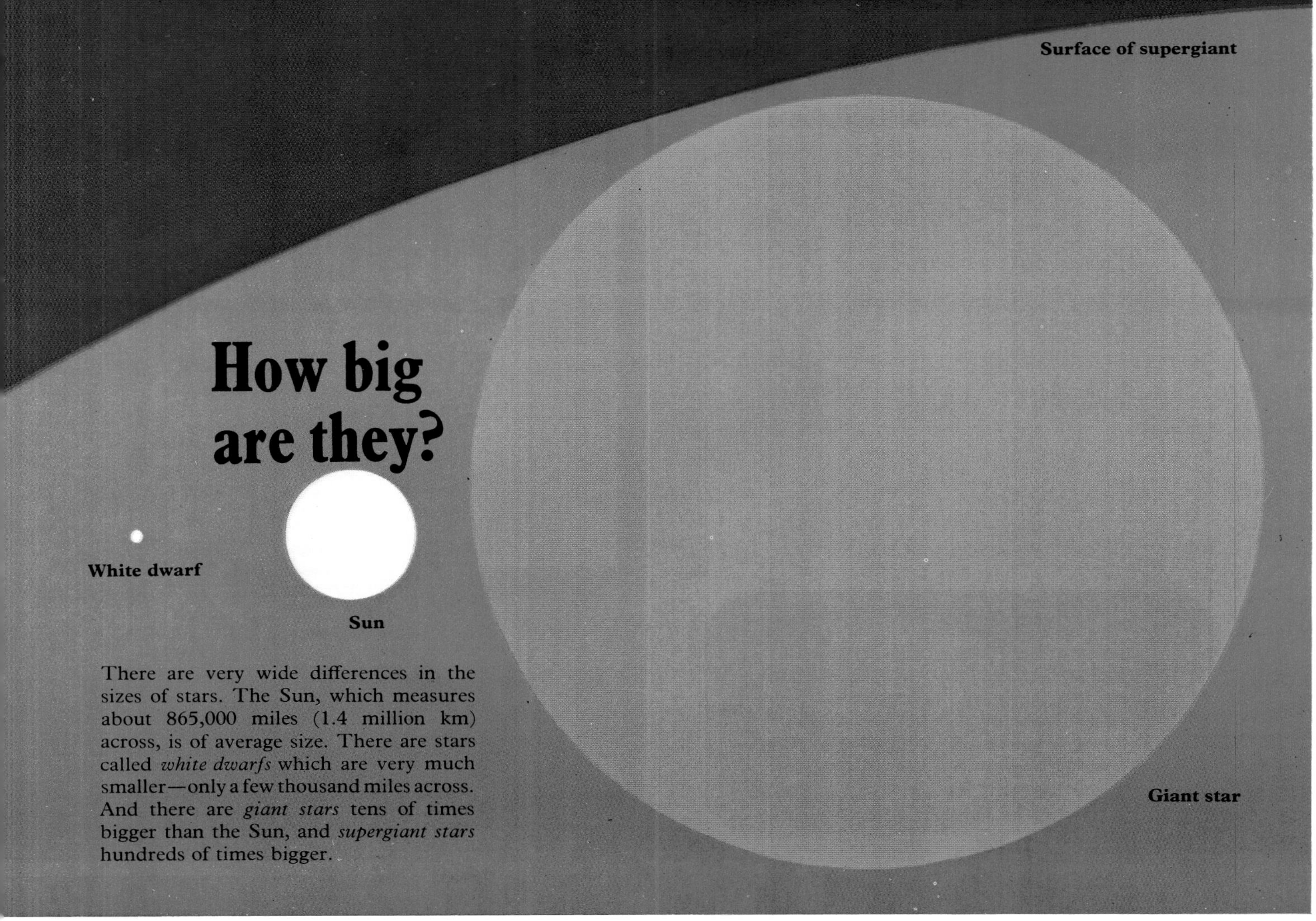

There are very wide differences in the sizes of stars. The Sun, which measures about 865,000 miles (1.4 million km) across, is of average size. There are stars called *white dwarfs* which are very much smaller—only a few thousand miles across. And there are *giant stars* tens of times bigger than the Sun, and *supergiant stars* hundreds of times bigger.

What is a double star?

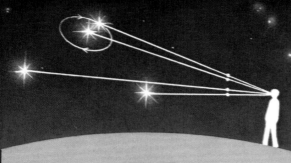

A *double star* is one which on closer inspection turns out to be two stars close together. They may only appear close together but actually be far apart. Or they may really be close together. Then they form a *binary system*.

Is the space between the stars empty?

Vast distances separate the stars in the heavens. But this space is not completely empty. It contains small amounts of dust and gas. In places, thicker clouds of dust and gas appear. We call them *nebulae* ("clouds"). Some nebulae shine brightly. Others appear dark, because they block the light of stars behind them.

STAR GROUPS The patterns of bright stars we call the constellations help us find our way through the heavens. The stars in the constellations appear to lie close together in space. But this is not really the case. They lie at different distances, and only appear close together because they are in the same direction when we look at them. However, stars do congregate together in space. In fact only one star in every three journeys through space alone. The Sun is one of them. On a wider scale, all the stars you see in the sky belong to the same star system, or galaxy. And on a wider scale still, galaxies tend to group together in space.

What is a star cluster?

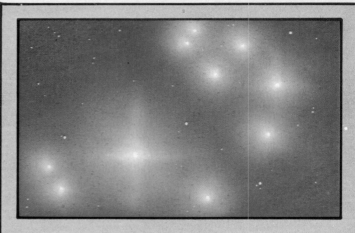

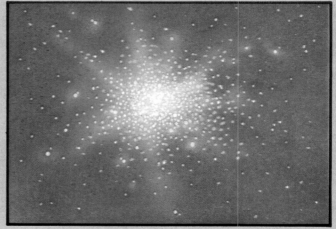

In a binary star system, the two stars revolve around each other. There are also *multiple star systems* in which three or more stars circle around each other. On a larger scale, tens and even hundreds of stars may cluster together in space to form loose *open clusters*. Sometimes several thousand stars form a closely packed *globular cluster*.

What is the Milky Way?

On dark nights, you often see a faint band of light arcing across the sky. We call it the *Milky Way*. If you look at it with binoculars, you see that it consists of thousands of stars. It represents a slice through our galaxy.

What is our galaxy like?

We also call our galaxy the *Milky Way*. It is a huge disk of stars, which has a dense center and has arms curving out from it. The whole disk revolves, somewhat like a Catherine wheel. From one side to the other, our galaxy measures about one million million million miles, or about 100,000 light-years.

Are all galaxies the same?

Our own galaxy has curved arms coming from a dense center. It is called a *spiral galaxy*. There are many spiral galaxies in the universe. Some galaxies have no distinct arms, and are called *elliptical* (oval) *galaxies*. Other galaxies are shapeless, or *irregular*.

THE OUTER GALAXIES Millions upon millions of miles beyond our own galaxy—the Milky Way—lie other galaxies. Many of them are similar to our own, and contain a similar number of stars—about 100,000 million. They are, on average, about the same size too—about 100,000 light-years in diameter. They also contain the same kinds of heavenly bodies as our own galaxy. Space and all the galaxies within it make up what we call the universe. Some of the galaxies astronomers can see through their telescopes are so far away that their light takes thousands of millions of years to reach us. This means that we are seeing them as they were thousands of millions of years ago.

Can we see any with the naked eye?

Most galaxies are so far away that they can be seen only through telescopes. But one or two are just visible to the naked eye. One is the famous Andromeda galaxy. This is visible as a misty patch in the constellation of Andromeda. It is often called the *Andromeda Nebula*.

Which is the closest?

The closest galaxy lies in the far southern heavens. It is clearly visible as a distinct cloud. And it is called the *Large Magellanic Cloud*. Nearby is the *Small Magellanic Cloud*, another close galaxy. They are named after the famous Portuguese navigator Ferdinand Magellan.

Are the galaxies moving?

Everything in the universe moves. The stars spin around the center of their galaxy. And the galaxy moves bodily through space. Viewed from the Earth, almost all the galaxies appear to be moving away from us. The farthest appear to be traveling fastest.

How did the universe begin?

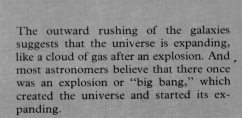

The outward rushing of the galaxies suggests that the universe is expanding, like a cloud of gas after an explosion. And most astronomers believe that there once was an explosion or "big bang," which created the universe and started its expanding.

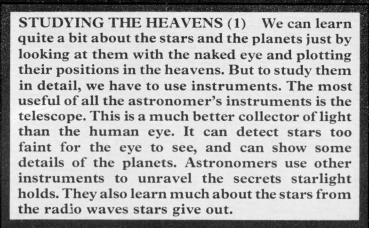

STUDYING THE HEAVENS (1) We can learn quite a bit about the stars and the planets just by looking at them with the naked eye and plotting their positions in the heavens. But to study them in detail, we have to use instruments. The most useful of all the astronomer's instruments is the telescope. This is a much better collector of light than the human eye. It can detect stars too faint for the eye to see, and can show some details of the planets. Astronomers use other instruments to unravel the secrets starlight holds. They also learn much about the stars from the radio waves stars give out.

Where do astronomers work?

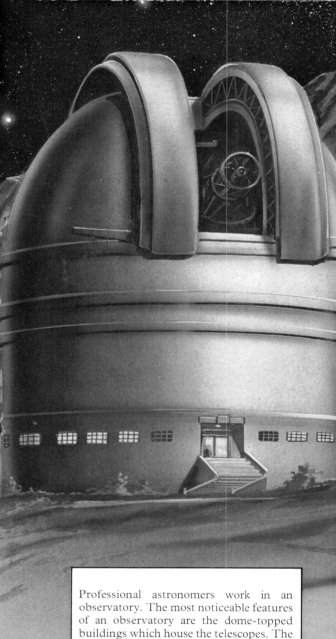

What kinds of telescopes do they use?

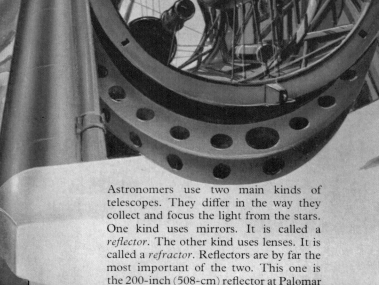

Astronomers use two main kinds of telescopes. They differ in the way they collect and focus the light from the stars. One kind uses mirrors. It is called a *reflector*. The other kind uses lenses. It is called a *refractor*. Reflectors are by far the most important of the two. This one is the 200-inch (508-cm) reflector at Palomar Observatory in California.

Professional astronomers work in an observatory. The most noticeable features of an observatory are the dome-topped buildings which house the telescopes. The domes roll back at night to expose the telescopes. Most major observatories are located away from the cities, high up in the mountains in sunny climates. There, the air is thinner and free from dust. This enables much clearer viewing.

How do reflectors work?

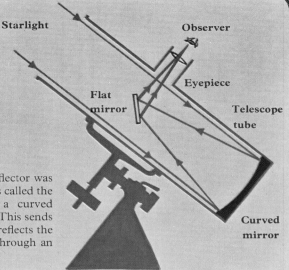

The most important type of reflector was devised by Isaac Newton, and is called the *Newtonian reflector*. It uses a curved mirror to gather the light rays. This sends the rays to a flat mirror, which reflects the light into the observer's eyes through an eyepiece.

How do refractors work?

The refractor consists of two sets of lenses held in a tube. At the front is the object lens and at the rear is the eyepiece. The eyepiece can be moved in and out for focusing. Most refractors are not as good as reflectors because they absorb light and may distort the image.

Are binoculars any use in astronomy?

Binoculars are very useful—especially for the amateur astronomer. They are inexpensive, and enable the observer to see many more interesting objects than can be seen with the naked eye. The Moon is a great sight through binoculars. And binoculars are ideal for comet watching. Many comets have been found recently by amateurs with binoculars.

Why is photography important in astronomy?

Astronomers at the big observatories rarely look through their telescopes. Instead, they use them as big cameras to take photographs of the night sky. Photographic film stores the light that falls on it, so if you point a telescope at the same part of the sky for hours on end, very faint stars will make their mark on the film.

What does starlight tell us?

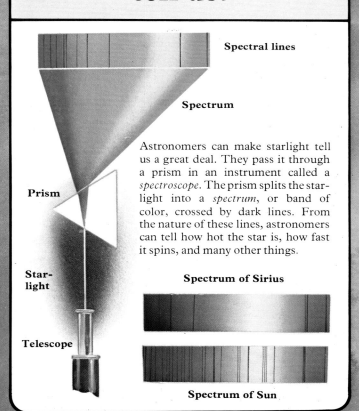

Spectral lines

Spectrum

Prism

Star-light

Telescope

Astronomers can make starlight tell us a great deal. They pass it through a prism in an instrument called a *spectroscope*. The prism splits the starlight into a *spectrum*, or band of color, crossed by dark lines. From the nature of these lines, astronomers can tell how hot the star is, how fast it spins, and many other things.

Spectrum of Sirius

Spectrum of Sun

At the Planetarium

If you are interested in astronomy, you should go to a planetarium. There, you will see how and why the stars change from season to season; how the planets and the Moon move through the heavens; and many other things. You sit in a chamber with a domed roof, onto which all the heavenly bodies can be projected.

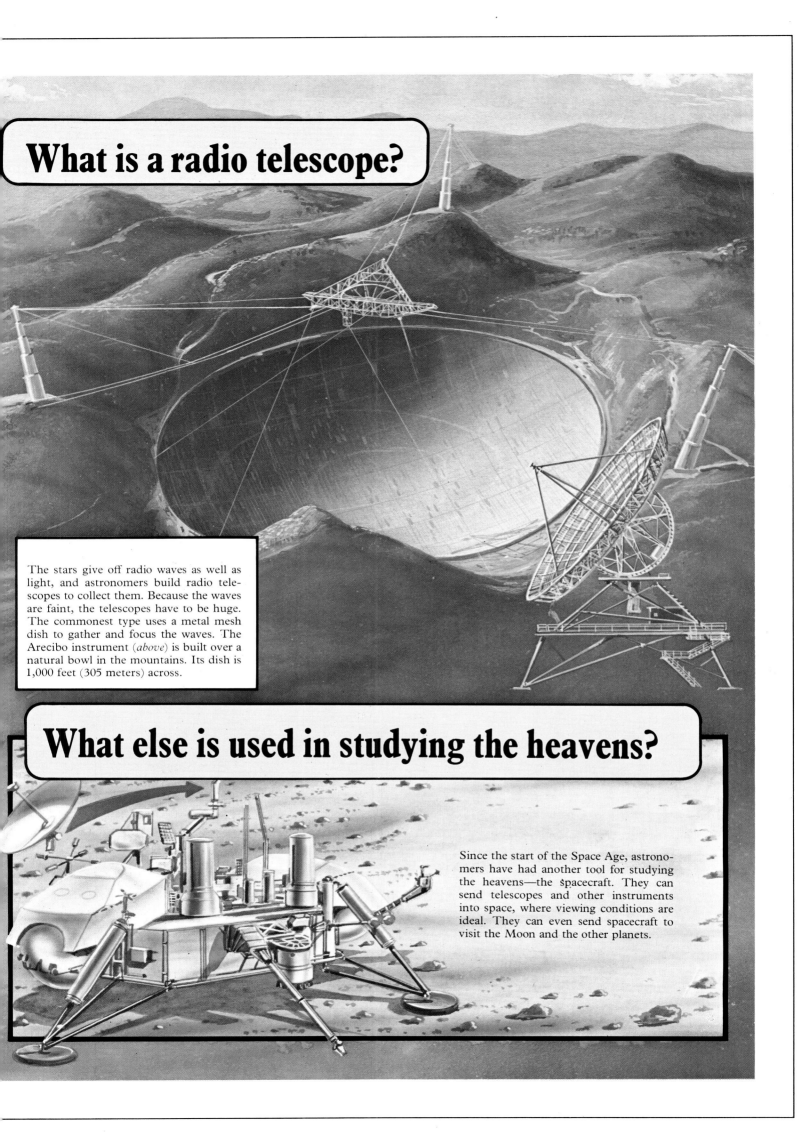

What is a radio telescope?

The stars give off radio waves as well as light, and astronomers build radio telescopes to collect them. Because the waves are faint, the telescopes have to be huge. The commonest type uses a metal mesh dish to gather and focus the waves. The Arecibo instrument (*above*) is built over a natural bowl in the mountains. Its dish is 1,000 feet (305 meters) across.

What else is used in studying the heavens?

Since the start of the Space Age, astronomers have had another tool for studying the heavens—the spacecraft. They can send telescopes and other instruments into space, where viewing conditions are ideal. They can even send spacecraft to visit the Moon and the other planets.

A-Z of Stars and Planets

A

Andromeda A constellation.
Aquarius, the Water-Bearer. A constellation.
Aquila, the Eagle. A constellation.
Ara, the Altar. A constellation.
Aries, the Ram. A constellation.
artificial satellite An artificial object that circles around the Earth in space.
asteroid A tiny planet-like body that circles around the Sun.
astrology Studying the stars to try to foretell the future.
astronaut A space traveler; literally "startraveler."
atmosphere The layer of gases around a heavenly body.
Auriga, the Charioteer. A constellation.
aurora A glow that appears in far northern and southern night skies. Commonly called the northern or southern lights.

B

Böotes, the Herdsman. A constellation.

C

calendar A means of splitting up time; it organizes the days, weeks, and months into years.
Cancer, the Crab. A constellation.
Canis Major, the Great Dog. A constellation.
Canis Minor, the Little Dog. A constellation.
Capricornus, the Sea Goat. A constellation.
Carina, the Keel. A constellation.
Cassiopeia A constellation.
celestial sphere An imaginary globe surrounding the Earth, to which all the stars appear to be fixed.
Centaurus, the Centaur. A constellation.
Cetus, the Whale. A constellation.
comet A ball of dust and gas that circles the Sun.
constellation A pattern bright stars make in the sky.
cosmic rays Streams of particles that bombard the Earth from space.
cosmos Another word for "universe."
crater A hole made when a lump of rock from space hits a planet or a moon.

Crux, the Southern Cross. A constellation.
Cygnus, the Swan. A constellation.

D

double star A star that looks like a single star to the eye, but is actually made up of two stars close together.
Draco, the Dragon. A constellation.

E

eclipse What happens when one heavenly body passes in front of another and blots out its light.
equinox One of two times of the year when the lengths of the day and night are equal. The vernal (spring) equinox occurs on about March 21st, and the autumnal equinox occurs on about September 23rd.
Eridanus A constellation.

G

galaxy A great spinning star island in space.
Gemini, the Twins. A constellation.
gravity A powerful force which makes bodies attract one another. The Earth's gravity keeps us firmly on the ground.

H

Hercules A constellation.
horoscope A diagram used in astrology showing the positions of the heavenly bodies when a person was born.
Hydra, the Water Serpent. A constellation.

I

interstellar space Space outside the solar system and among the stars.

L

Leo, the Lion. A constellation.
Libra, the Scales. A constellation.
light-year The distance light travels in a year—about 6 million million miles or 10 million million km.
lunar Of the Moon.
Lyra, the Lyre. A constellation.

M

magnitude A scale of star brightness. The brightest stars you can see with the naked eye are of the 1st magnitude; the faintest are of the 6th magnitude.
mare One of the dark areas on the Moon; means "sea."
meteor A streak of light in the sky, caused when tiny rocks burn up in the Earth's atmosphere.
moon A body that orbits around a planet; properly called "satellite."

N

nebula A cloud of dust and gas in space.
nova A faint star that suddenly flares up and appears "new."
nuclear reaction A process in which atoms either split or combine together, producing tremendous energy. Stars get their energy when hydrogen atoms combine.

O

observatory A place where astronomers study the stars.
Ophiuchus, the Serpent Bearer. A constellation.
orbit The path in space of a body when it travels around another.
Orion A constellation.

P

Pegasus, the Winged Horse. A constellation.
period An interval of time between the beginning and end of something, such as an orbit.
Perseus A constellation.
phase The apparent change in shape of the Moon or a planet as more or less of its surface is lit by the Sun.
Pisces, the Fishes. A constellation.
Plough The name for the pattern made by the seven brightest stars in the constellation Ursa Major.
pole star The star Polaris, which lies almost directly above the north pole and does not appear to move.
pulsar A tiny star that gives out its energy in rapid bursts or pulses.
Puppis, the Poop. A constellation.

Q

quasar A mysterious, distant heavenly body that gives out powerful radio waves.

R

radio astronomy A branch of astronomy which studies the radio waves stars and galaxies give out.
red giant A huge, cool red star that may be hundreds of times bigger than the Sun.
reflector A telescope that collects light with a curved mirror.
refractor A telescope that collects light with lenses.

S

Sagittarius, the Archer. A constellation.
satellite A small body that circles around a planet; a moon.
season A regular change in climate that occurs because the Earth's axis is tilted in space.
Serpens, the Serpent. A constellation.
Scorpio, the Scorpion. A constellation.
shooting star Another term for meteor.
solar Of the Sun.
solstice A time of the year when the Sun appears farthest north or south of the Equator. In northern parts of the Earth, for example, it is mid-summer when the Sun appears farthest north (about June 21st); it is mid-winter when the Sun appears farthest south (December 21st).
spectrum The band of color formed when light passes through a prism. Astronomers can tell much about a star from the spectrum of its light.
stellar Of the stars.
sundial A kind of clock that tells time according to the position of the Sun.
supergiant A huge star many hundreds or even thousands of times bigger than the Sun.
supernova A star that flares up brilliantly as it explodes.

T

Taurus, the Bull. A constellation.
telescope An instrument for observing distant objects, such as the stars and planets.
terrestrial Of the Earth.
tides The regular rise and fall of the oceans caused by the Moon's gravity.
transit The passage of Mercury or Venus across the disk of the Sun.

U

universe All that exists—space and all the bodies within it.
Ursa Major, the Great Bear. A constellation.
Ursa Minor, the Little Bear. A constellation.

V

Vela, the Sails. A constellation.
Virgo, the Virgin. A constellation.

W

white dwarf A tiny but very heavy star that is near the end of its life.

Z

zodiac A band of the heavens through which the Sun and the planets appear to move during the year. The signs of the zodiac are the signs of the constellations the band passes through.

Famous Astronomers

Aristarchus (200 BC) Greek who first proposed that the Earth travels around the Sun.
Brahe, Tycho (1546–1601) Great Danish observer who built a famous observatory on Hveen, in the Baltic.
Copernicus, Nicolaus (1473–1543) Polish priest-astronomer who founded modern astronomy with his idea of a Sun-centered universe.
Einstein, Albert (1879–1955) German physicist who put forward the theory of relativity that changed our ideas of space, time, and motion.
Galileo (1564–1642) Italian who first used a telescope to observe the heavens.
Halley, Edmond (1656–1742) Englishman particularly famed for his studies of comets, including the one named after him.
Herschel, William (1738–1822) German-born astronomer who settled in England; discovered the planet Uranus in 1781.
Hipparchus (100 BC) The greatest Greek astronomer, who drew up star catalogues and discovered trigonometry.
Hoyle, Fred (1915–) English astronomer best known for his "steady-state" theory of the origin of the universe.
Hubble, Edwin (1899–1953) American who pioneered the study of the outer galaxies.
Jansky, Karl (1905–1950) American radio engineer who first detected radio waves from the heavens, and thus founded radio astronomy.
Kepler, Johannes (1571–1630) German who first described how the planets moved—in ellipses.
Lemaître, Georges (1894–1966) One of the first to develop the "big-bang" theory about how the universe began.
Messier, Charles (1730–1817) Frenchman who compiled a list of nebulae and clusters. Many are still identified by their M-numbers.
Newton, Isaac (1642–1727) Brilliant Englishman who discovered the laws of gravity and motion and built the first reflecting telescope.
Ptolemy (AD 150's) Greek who wrote the first astronomical work, the *Almagest* ("The Greatest").
Schiaparelli, Giovanni (1835–1910) Italian who said he observed canals on Mars, which led people to believe that there might be life on that planet.

THE SOLAR SYSTEM

Name	Distance from Sun miles (km)	Diameter at Equator miles (km)	Density (water = 1)	*Turns on axis in	†Circles Sun in
Sun	—	865,000 (1,392,000)	1.4	25 days	—
Moon	—	2,160 (3,476)	3.3	27 days	—
Mercury	36,000,000 (58,000,000)	3,015 (4,850)	5.4	59 days	88 days
Venus	67,000,000 (108,000,000)	7,545 (12,140)	5.2	244 days	225 days
Earth	93,000,000 (150,000,000)	7,926 (12,756)	5.5	23h 56min	365¼ days
Mars	142,000,000 (228,000,000)	4,220 (6,790)	4.0	24h 37min	687 days
Jupiter	484,000,000 (778,000,000)	88,600 (142,600)	1.3	9h 50min	12 years
Saturn	887,000,000 (1,427,000,000)	74,700 (120,200)	0.7	10h 14min	30 years
Uranus	1,783,000,000 (2,870,000,000)	30,500 (49,000)	1.6	10h 49min	84 years
Neptune	2,794,000,000 (4,497,000,000)	31,200 (50,200)	2.3	15h 48min	165 years
Pluto	3,670,000,000 (5,900,000,000)	3,980 (6,400)	?	6 days	248 years

*This is the planet's day.   †This is the planet's year.

THE BRIGHTEST STARS

Name	Constellation	Distance (light-years)
Sirius	Canis Major	9
Canopus	Carina	200
Rigil Kent	Centaurus	4⅓
Arcturus	Boötes	40
Vega	Lyra	30
Capella	Auriga	50
Rigel	Orion	800
Procyon	Canis Minor	11
Achernar	Eridanus	130
Hadar	Centaurus	400
Altair	Aquila	16
Betelgeuse	Orion	650

THE NEAREST STARS

Name	Constellation	Distance (light-years)
Proxima Centauri	Centaurus	4.3
Rigil Kent	Centaurus	4.4
Barnard's Star	Ophiuchus	5.9
Wolf 359	Leo	7.6
Lalande 21185	Ursa Major	8.1
Sirius	Canis Major	8.8

NAMES OF THE CONSTELLATIONS

Latin name	English name	Latin name	English name	Latin name	English name
Andromeda	Andromeda	Delphinus	Dolphin	Pegasus	Pegasus (winged horse)
Antlia	Air Pump	Dorado	Swordfish		
Apus	Bird of Paradise	Draco	Dragon	Perseus	Perseus
Aquarius	Water Bearer	Equuleus	Little Horse	Phoenix	Phoenix
Aquila	Eagle	Eridanus	River Eridanus	Pictor	Painter (or Easel)
Ara	Altar	Fornax	Furnace	Pisces	Fishes
Aries	Ram	Gemini	Twins	Piscis Austrinus	Southern Fish
Auriga	Charioteer	Grus	Crane	Puppis	Poop
Boötes	Herdsman	Hercules	Hercules	Pyxis	Mariner's Compass
Caelum	Chisel	Horologium	Clock	Reticulum	Net
Camelopardus	Giraffe	Hydra	Sea-Serpent	Sagitta	Arrow
Cancer	Crab	Hydrus	Watersnake	Sagittarius	Archer
Canes Venatici	Hunting Dogs	Indus	Indian	Scorpius	Scorpion
Canis Major	Great Dog	Lacerta	Lizard	Sculptor	Sculptor
Canis Minor	Little Dog	Leo	Lion	Scutum	Shield
Capricornus	Sea-Goat	Leo Minor	Little Lion	Serpens	Serpent
Carina	Keel	Lepus	Hare	Sextans	Sextant
Cassiopeia	Cassiopeia	Libra	Scales	Taurus	Bull
Centaurus	Centaur	Lupus	Wolf	Telescopium	Telescope
Cepheus	Cepheus	Lynx	Lynx	Triangulum	Triangle
Cetus	Whale	Lyra	Lyre	Triangulum Australe	Southern Triangle
Chamaeleon	Chameleon	Mensa	Table		
Circinus	Pair of Compasses	Microscopium	Microscope	Tucana	Toucan
Columba	Dove	Monoceros	Unicorn	Ursa Major	Great Bear (or Plough)
Coma Berenices	Berenice's Hair	Musca	Fly		
Corona Australis	Southern Crown	Norma	Rule	Ursa Minor	Little Bear
Corona Borealis	Northern Crown	Octans	Octant	Vela	Sails
Corvus	Crow	Ophiuchus	Serpent Bearer	Virgo	Virgin
Crater	Cup	Orion	Orion (hunter)	Volans	Flying Fish
Crux	Southern Cross	Pavo	Peacock	Vulpecula	Fox
Cygnus	Swan				

Our Planet Earth

How did ancient peoples see the world?

From Hindu legends, we know that Indians once thought that the Earth looked like the drawing above. They thought that the Earth rested on a golden plate supported by elephants. The elephants stood on a turtle, representing the water god, Vishnu.

PLANET EARTH Early peoples based many of their ideas about the Earth on superstitions. But we now understand that the Earth is a planet in the solar system, which is rotating around the center of the Milky Way galaxy. The Earth also rotates around the Sun, at the same time spinning on its own axis. Day and night occur alternately as part of the Earth faces the Sun and is then turned away from it. And, because the Earth's axis is tilted, we have seasons.

Where is the Earth in the solar system?

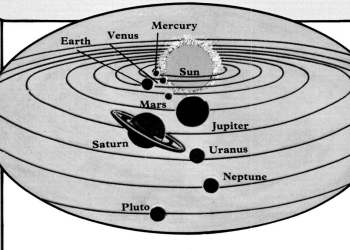

The Earth is the third planet from the Sun. Only Mercury and Venus are closer to the Sun. Apart from the nine planets, the solar system also contains moons, meteorites, comets, asteroids, gas, and dust.

What is the Earth's axis?

The Earth's axis is an imaginary line joining the North Pole, the center of the Earth, and the South Pole. The axis is tilted at $66\frac{1}{2}°$ to the plane of the Earth's orbit. The average time taken by the Earth to spin once on its axis is about 24 hours, or one complete day.

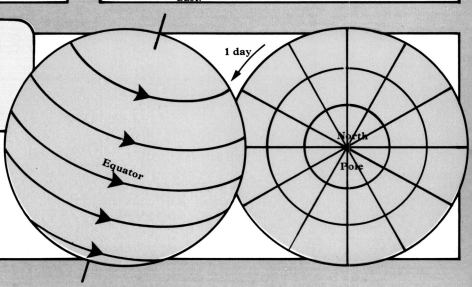

Is time the same everywhere on Earth?

On Earth, 15° of longitude represents 1 hour's time difference, because 15° × 24 hours equals 360°—the number of degrees in a circle. Time zones are modified to prevent a small country having two times.

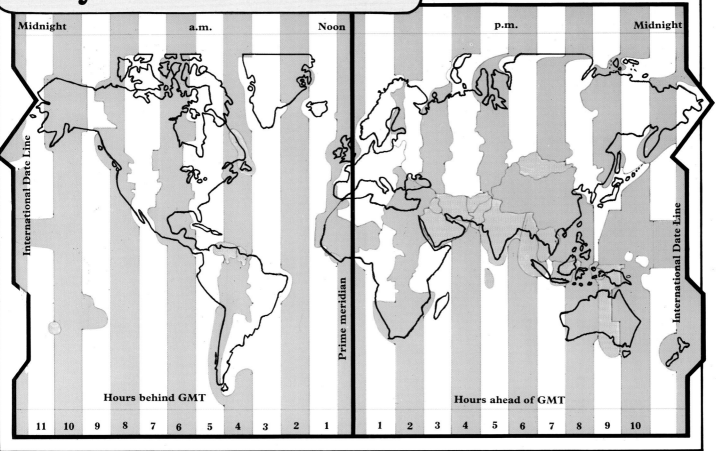

Midnight   a.m.   Noon   p.m.   Midnight

International Date Line

Prime meridian

International Date Line

Hours behind GMT

Hours ahead of GMT

| 11 | 10 | 9 | 8 | 7 | 6 | 5 | 4 | 3 | 2 | 1 | | 1 | 2 | 3 | 4 | 5 | 6 | 7 | 8 | 9 | 10 |

Why are there seasons?

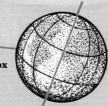

Spring equinox
N. Hemisphere
Autumn equinox
S. Hemisphere
March 21

Summer solstice
N. Hemisphere
Winter solstice
S. Hemisphere
June 21

Winter solstice
N. Hemisphere
Summer solstice
S. Hemisphere
December 21

Autumn equinox
N. Hemisphere
Spring equinox
S. Hemisphere
September 23

At the equinoxes, the Sun is overhead at the Equator. It is overhead at the Tropic of Cancer (23°27′N) or the Tropic of Capricorn (23°27′S) at the solstices. This changing position of the overhead Sun explains why we have seasons.

How was the solar system formed?

Most scientists think that, 5,000 million years ago, our Solar System was a mass of gas and dust (top). This material contracted to form the Sun (center) and the planets (bottom) about 4,550 million years ago.

THE EARTH WE LIVE ON   Our planet Earth was formed about 4,550 million years ago, probably from a cloud of gas and dust that was drifting around the newly created Sun. As the Earth formed, heavier materials, such as iron, sank toward the core. Lighter materials rose and hardened to form the thin crust. Today, oceans cover more than seven-tenths of the Earth's surface. But the land is extremely varied, from mountain ranges to plains.

What is the Earth's interior like?

Facts and Figures About the Earth
Size The diameter of the Earth at the Equator is 7,926 miles (12,756 km).
But the Earth is not a true sphere. The diameter from pole to pole is 7,899 miles (12,713 km).
Mass 5,882 million million million tons.
Area 196,937,600 sq miles (510,066,000 sq km).
Land Area About 29 per cent of the Earth's surface.
Highest peak on land Everest, 29,028 feet (8,848 m) above sea level.
Water area About 71 per cent of the Earth's surface.
Deepest point in the oceans 36,198 feet (11,033 m) in the Marianas Trench, in the Pacific Ocean. The deepest descent was 35,820 feet (10,918 m) in 1960.
Highest recorded air temperature 136.4°F (58.0°C), in Libya in 1922.
Lowest recorded air temperature—126.9°F (—88.3°C), recorded in Antarctica (1960).

Inner core

Outer core

Mantle

Crust

The Earth's crust is only a thin shell, between 4 and 37 miles (6 and 60 km) thick. Beneath the crust is the dense mantle, which is 1,800 miles (2,900 km) thick. The core's diameter is about 4,300 miles (6,920 km). The outer core is liquid, but the extremely dense inner core is solid.

How much of the Earth is covered by water?

These two views of the Earth show how much of its surface is covered by water. The land hemisphere has its center between London and Berlin. The sea hemisphere has its center near New Zealand.

Which is the highest mountain?

We usually think of Mount Everest as the world's highest mountain. However, some volcanic peaks rise from the sea bed and surface as islands. One of them, Mauna Kea, in Hawaii, is 33,474 feet (10,203 m) high—measured from the ocean bed. But only 13,796 feet (4,205 m) is actually above sea level.

What is the highest point on land?

The highest point in the world is Mount Everest, in the Himalayas. It rises to a height of 29,028 feet (8,848 m) above sea level, on the borders of Nepal and Tibet, north of India. The Himalayan range has several peaks higher than 23,000 feet (7,000 m). It is known as the "Roof of the World."

What is the lowest point on land?

The Dead Sea is an extremely salty lake between Israel and Jordan. Because it is so salty, people can float in it without sinking. The shore of the Dead Sea is the lowest point on land anywhere in the world. It is 1,289 feet (393 m) lower than the mean sea level of the Mediterranean Sea, which lies to the west.

What are the main divisions of Earth history?

EARTH HISTORY For the first 1,350 million years of Earth history, our planet was probably lifeless. The first simple plants appeared about 3,300 million years ago. Animal fossils are rare in the older rocks, probably because animals were soft-bodied, like jellyfish and worms. By about 570 million years ago, however, many creatures had developed hard parts, which were preserved as fossils. Geologists have divided the last 570 million years into eras—the Paleozoic, Mesozoic, and Cenozoic. Each era is divided into periods and some periods into epochs.

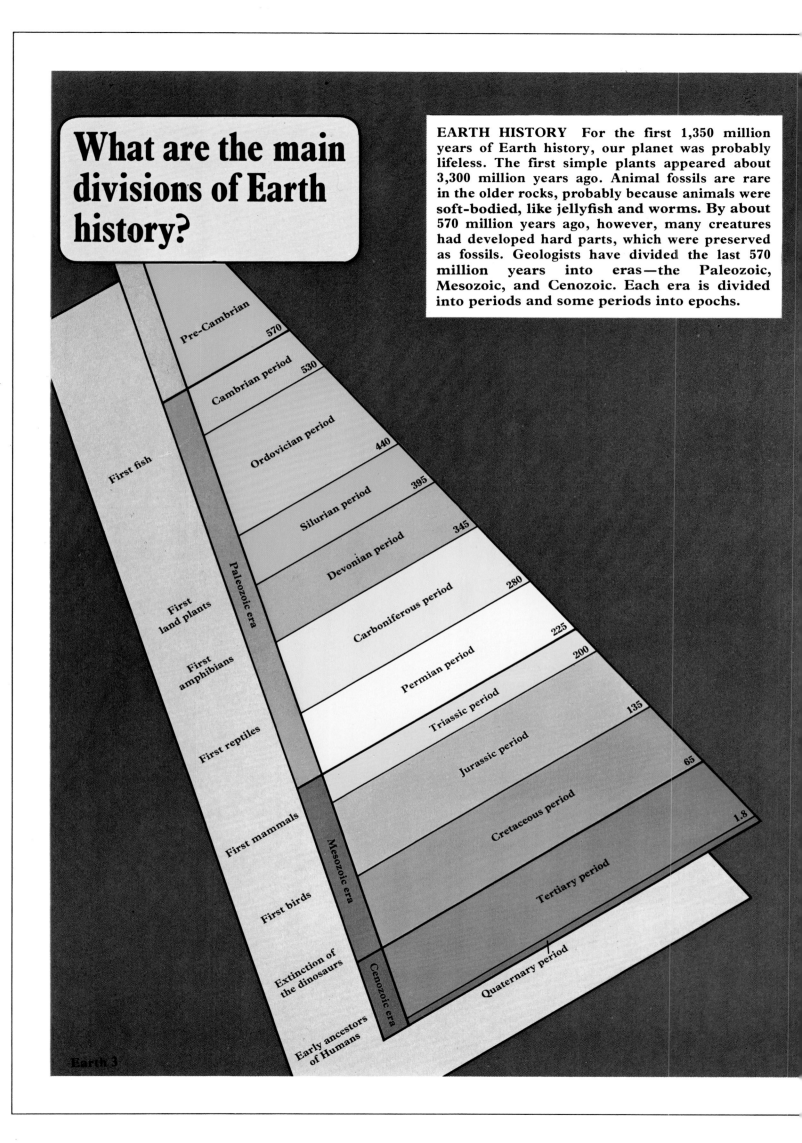

Pre-Cambrian 570

Cambrian period 530

Ordovician period 440

Silurian period 395

Devonian period 345

Carboniferous period 280

Permian period 225

Triassic period 200

Jurassic period 135

Cretaceous period 65

Tertiary period 1.8

Quaternary period

Paleozoic era

Mesozoic era

Cenozoic era

First fish

First land plants

First amphibians

First reptiles

First mammals

First birds

Extinction of the dinosaurs

Early ancestors of Humans

What were early fish like?

The latest evidence suggests that fish may have first appeared in the late Cambrian period. These strange fish were protected by armor, in the form of bony plates.

The first land animals, the amphibians, appeared in the Devonian period. They probably evolved from air-breathing fish. But amphibians were not true land animals, because they had to return to water to breed. Their descendants, the reptiles, were the first true land animals.

What were the first land animals like?

What did the first bird look like?

The first bird, *Archaeopteryx*, appeared in the Jurassic period. It had many reptilian features, such as its sharp teeth and its bony tail, much like a lizard's.

What was the biggest prehistoric animal?

Dinosaurs lived between 225 and 65 million years ago. They were an extremely varied animal group. The heaviest, *Stegosaurus*, may have weighed 100 tons.

What did human ancestors look like?

Ramapithecus was a human-like ape that appeared about 14 million years ago. Scientists have discovered from fossils of jaw and teeth that it had certain human features, and regard it as our earliest ancestor. There is a long gap in the fossil records before the appearance of the first undisputed members of the family, the australopithecines (southern apes). These emerged in southern and eastern Africa about 5 million years ago.

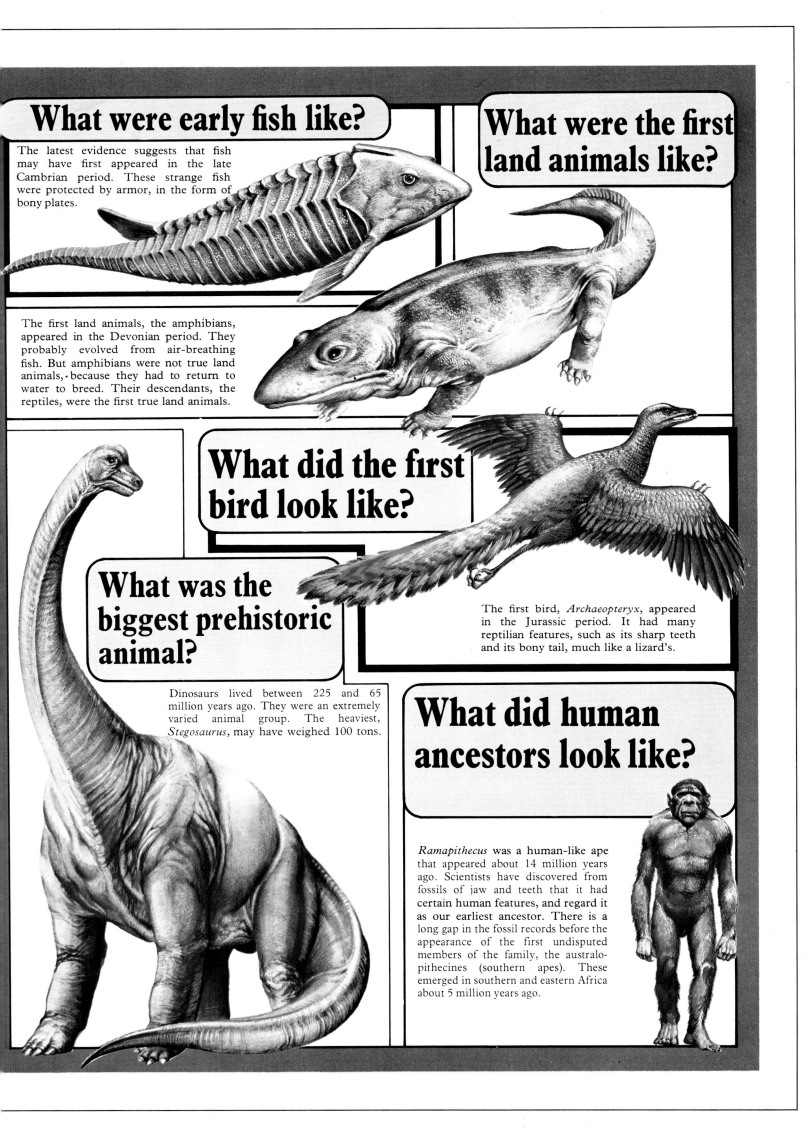

What happens where the continents meet the oceans?

Continental shelf

Continental slope

Coasts are not the true edges of the continents. Beyond the coasts is a shallow, gently sloping continental shelf, which is part of the continent. The continent really ends where the continental slope plunges steeply down to the oceanic abyss.

DRIFTING CONTINENTS

DRIFTING CONTINENTS The ground under our feet may seem firm. But it is actually moving, although the movement is slow. The Earth's crust is divided into several large areas, called "plates," which are separated by huge cracks. These plates move in two main ways. In places, hot, fluid mantle rock beneath the plates is rising and spreading, moving the plates along. And new rock is being added to the crust along underwater mountain ranges, called mid-oceanic ridges. This steady addition of new rock is pushing apart the plates on either side.

What is a plate?

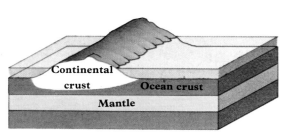

Continental crust   **Ocean crust**

Mantle

The plates in the Earth's crust are made up of the thin ocean crust and the continents that rest upon it. Beneath the ocean crust is the dense mantle. The top of the mantle is partly fluid. Currents in this fluid rock make the plates move.

Were the continents always separate?

North America

South America

Africa   **Europe**

The edges of the continental shelves, the true edges of the continents, have been mapped. Scientists have found that the edges of the continental shelves of the Americas fit together with those of Europe and Africa like pieces in a giant jigsaw. This shows that the continents were probably once joined together.

Does the sea bed show evidence of continental drift?

In the oceans, there are huge mountain ranges called *mid-oceanic ridges*. Scientists have discovered that new rock is being added along the center of these ridges. As a result, the oceans are being widened.

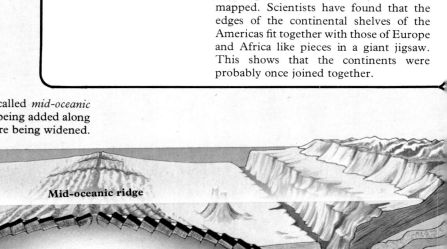

Mid-oceanic ridge

Is there any other evidence?

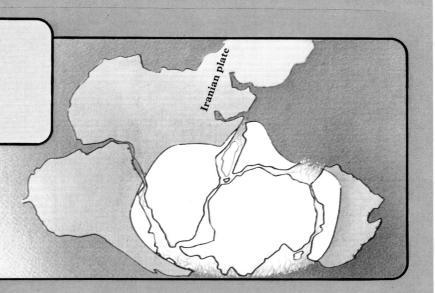

About 290 million years ago, there was a great Ice Age in the Southern Hemisphere. Studies of this Ice Age suggest that the continents were then joined, as the map shows. Fossils of the same animals and plants occur in the continents. This evidence also supports the theory.

What are the chief plates in the Earth's crust?

Below: Four views of the Earth show the main plates in the Earth's crust. Some of these plates are enormous, but some are fairly small. The plates are moving slowly. Near their edges are unstable areas, where volcanoes and earthquakes occur.

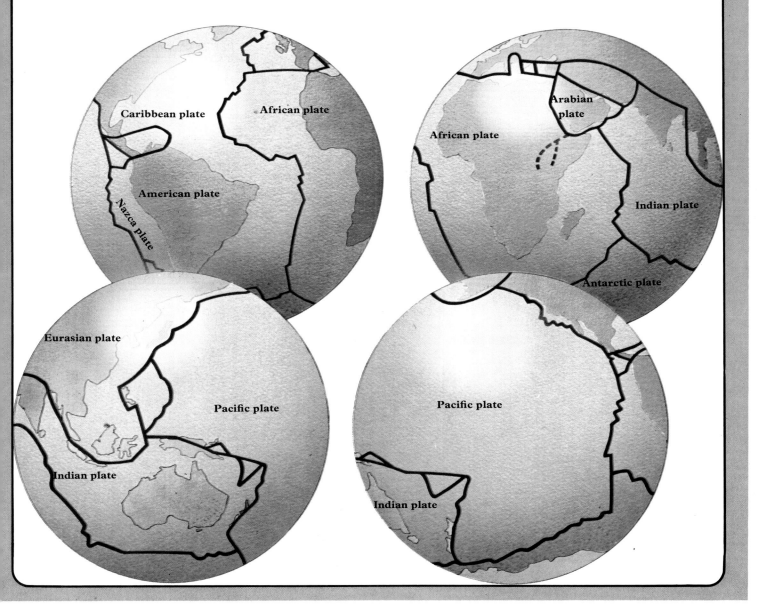

How did the continents move apart?

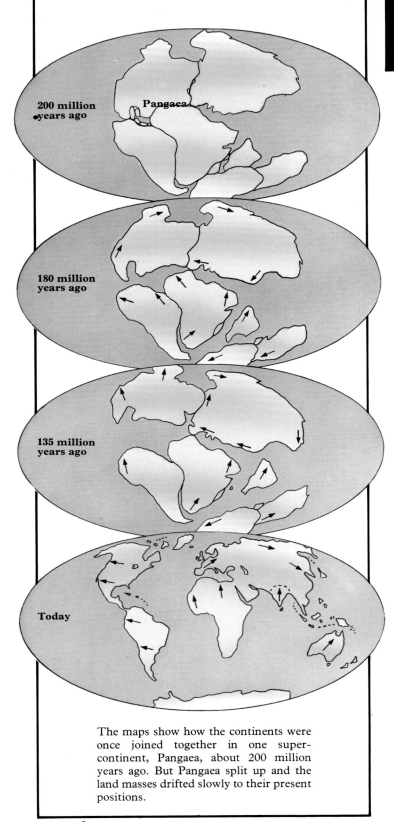

200 million years ago

Pangaea

180 million years ago

135 million years ago

Today

The maps show how the continents were once joined together in one super-continent, Pangaea, about 200 million years ago. But Pangaea split up and the land masses drifted slowly to their present positions.

CONTINENTS COLLIDE The plates in the crusts are moving by about three-fourths inch (2 cm) or less per year. But this movement has been going on for hundreds of millions of years. As a result, the continents have drifted apart over 200 million years. In places where plates are pushing against each other, crustal rock is being destroyed as one plate is pushed under the other. Sometimes, when two plates collide, the sediments between them are squeezed up into fold mountains.

What makes plates drift?

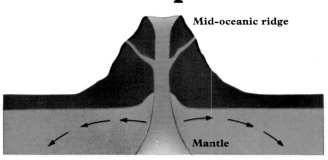

Mid-oceanic ridge

Mantle

The diagram shows molten rock rising to the surface along the mid-oceanic ridges. There it hardens and becomes new crustal rock. This widens the oceans. The diagram also shows currents in the mantle, which spread sideways, pushing the plates apart.

What are folds?

Evidence of the tremendous forces at work inside the Earth is shown in folded rocks. These rocks were formed in flat layers. But great lateral (sideways) pressure occurs when plates push against each other. The flat layers of rock are squeezed into great loops or folds.

What happens when plates collide?

When two plates push against each other, the edge of one plate is sometimes forced under the other. The descending plate edge is melted. Some of the melted rock may return to the surface through volcanoes.

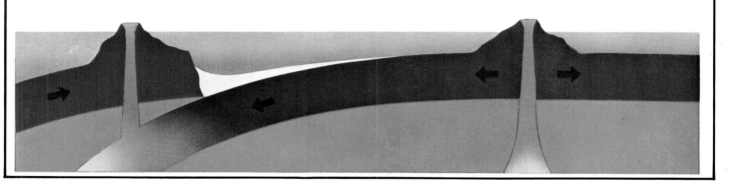

Does anything else happen?

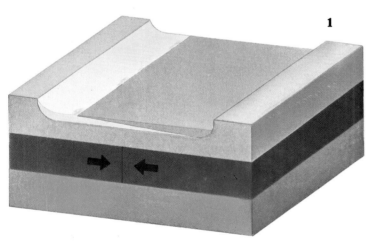

1

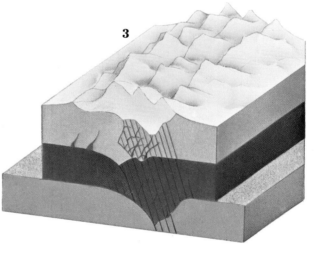

3

2

Sediments pile up on the floors of seas (1). These sediments consist of material worn from the land and the remains of sea animals and plants. Sometimes, when two plates are rammed together (2), the sediments are squeezed up into folds. Finally, the sea disappears and the plates are joined (3). The sediments form a new fold mountain range.

What is a fault?

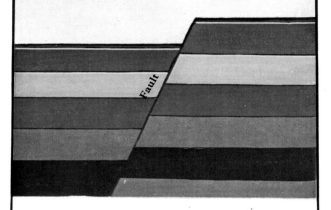

Faults are fractures, or cracks, in rock layers along which the rocks have moved. The movement is usually up and down, as shown above. After movement has occurred, the rock layers on either side of the fault do not match.

MOUNTAIN BUILDING Apart from fold mountains, there are two other main kinds of mountains. Block mountains are blocks of land that have been pushed up between faults in the Earth's crust. Volcanoes are mostly found near the edges of the crust's plates. Volcanoes are sometimes steep cones of volcanic ash. Others are lower but broader and are composed of layer upon layer of hardened lava. Some consist of alternate layers of ash and lava.

How are block mountains and rift valleys formed?

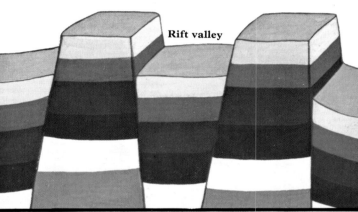

Block mountain

Rift valley

Vertical movements along faults create such features as block mountains, which are uplifted blocks of land, and rift valleys, where a block of land has slipped down between the faults. Small block mountains, which form ridges, are called *horsts*.

What are the main kinds of rock folds?

A simple up-fold in rocks is called an *anticline*. A simple down-fold is called a *syncline*. Some up-folds, such as the one on the left, contain many smaller folds. This complicated fold is called an *anticlinorium*. A *nappe* is a fold that has been bent over, broken away, and pushed along.

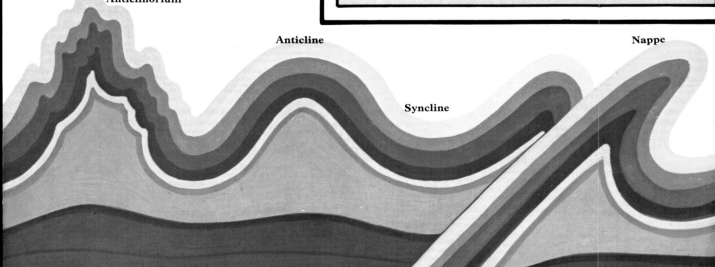

Anticlinorium

Anticline

Nappe

Syncline

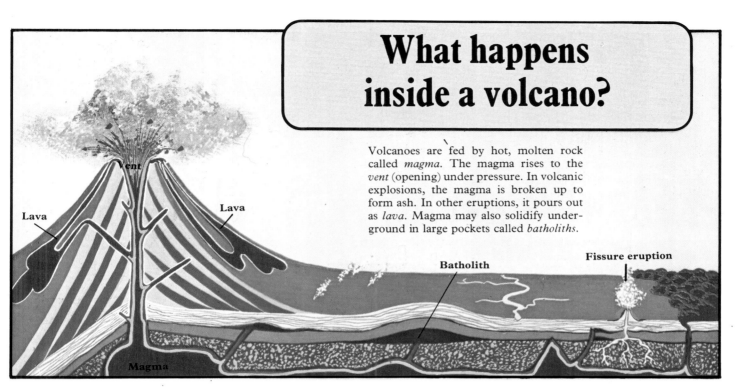

What happens inside a volcano?

Volcanoes are fed by hot, molten rock called *magma*. The magma rises to the *vent* (opening) under pressure. In volcanic explosions, the magma is broken up to form ash. In other eruptions, it pours out as *lava*. Magma may also solidify underground in large pockets called *batholiths*.

Vent

Lava

Lava

Batholith

Fissure eruption

Magma

What is lava like?

Lava is a terrifying sight as it advances toward a town. People have tried to cool and harden the lava by pumping water on it. But there is no real way of stopping its advance. People must wait until the eruption ends, and hope that their homes have not been destroyed by the lava.

VOLCANIC ERUPTIONS Some volcanoes erupt explosively. The lava inside the volcano and, sometimes, parts of the mountain itself, are shattered by explosive gases. Small pieces of hot volcanic ash or dust are shot into the air. They then rain down on surrounding areas, burning and burying fields and towns. In volcanoes where there is little gas, the eruptions are "quiet"—that is, streams of lava are emitted, but there is no explosion. Most volcanoes are intermediate, sometimes erupting explosively and sometimes quietly. Other features of volcanic regions are hot springs and geysers.

Do volcanoes contribute to life on Earth?

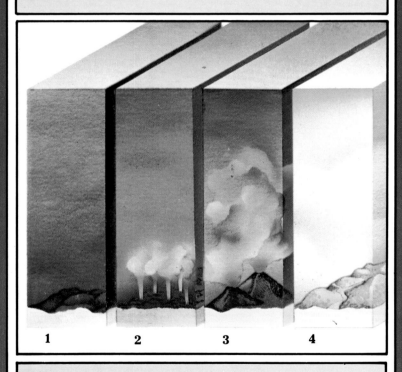

Volcanic action releases gases from the Earth's rocks. The first atmosphere (1), which was later lost into space, was created from the molten surface of the newly formed Earth. A new atmosphere was formed from lava and volcanoes (2 and 3). Then plants added oxygen, producing the mixture of air we breathe today (4).

Are there many kinds of volcanic eruptions?

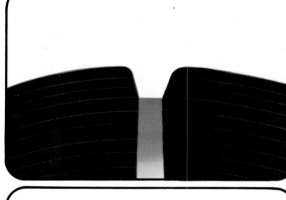

Top: Quiet volcanoes, such as those in Hawaii, are shaped like an upturned saucer. They emit lava and do not explode. *Center:* Explosive volcanoes are typified by Mt. Vesuvius in Italy, which erupted in AD 79. *Bottom: A nuée ardente,* or *glowing cloud* of hot gases, steam, and ash, is a feature of some volcanic explosions.

What were the effects of the famous Krakatoa eruption?

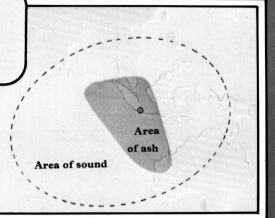

Krakatoa, a volcanic island between Java and Sumatra, was destroyed in 1883 by a great volcanic explosion. The sound was heard in Australia, thousands of miles away. Ash rained down on surrounding islands, which were also battered by a destructive wave, or *tsunami*.

Do volcanoes ever form new land?

Surtsey, a new volcanic island, appeared off Iceland in 1963. It rose from the mid-Atlantic ridge. Three weeks after it had surfaced, Surtsey was 400 feet (120 meters) high and nearly 0·6 mile (1 km) across.

Has a volcano ever buried an entire city?

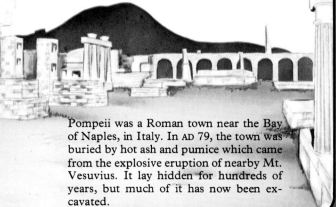

Pompeii was a Roman town near the Bay of Naples, in Italy. In AD 79, the town was buried by hot ash and pumice which came from the explosive eruption of nearby Mt. Vesuvius. It lay hidden for hundreds of years, but much of it has now been excavated.

Are geysers connected with volcanoes?

Geysers are types of hot springs that periodically erupt jets of hot water and steam into the air. They sometimes occur because underground water is heated to steam by magma in volcanic regions. The steam forces the water upward. Other geyser eruptions are caused by gases in the water.

What causes earthquakes?

EARTHQUAKES Most earthquakes are caused by rocks moving along faults. Earthquakes can occur anywhere. But they are most common and most severe near plate edges. The place where an earthquake originates is the focus, which is usually underground. The point on the surface directly above it is the epicenter. The strength of earthquakes is measured on the Richter scale, which is numbered from 1 to 9. A 2-point quake is barely noticeable. But a 7-point quake is severe.

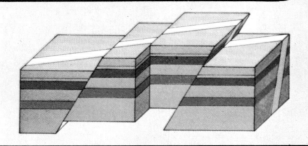

The movement along most faults is vertical. But movements may occur in any direction. For example, movements along some faults are horizontal—that is, the rocks move alongside each other. It is the sudden movements at faults that cause earthquakes.

Why is the San Andreas fault famous?

The San Andreas fault is in California, near the cities of Los Angeles and San Francisco. The fault is about 597 miles (960 km) long. It forms part of the boundary between the Pacific plate, which is moving north-westwards, and the American plate, which is moving south-eastwards.

What is the greatest disaster caused by the San Andreas fault?

Movements along the San Andreas fault are not smooth. The jagged edges of the plates become jammed together. The pressure then builds up until the jam breaks and the rocks lurch suddenly forward. A sudden movement in 1906 caused the San Francisco earthquake. Near the city, the fault moved 15 feet (4·6 meters).

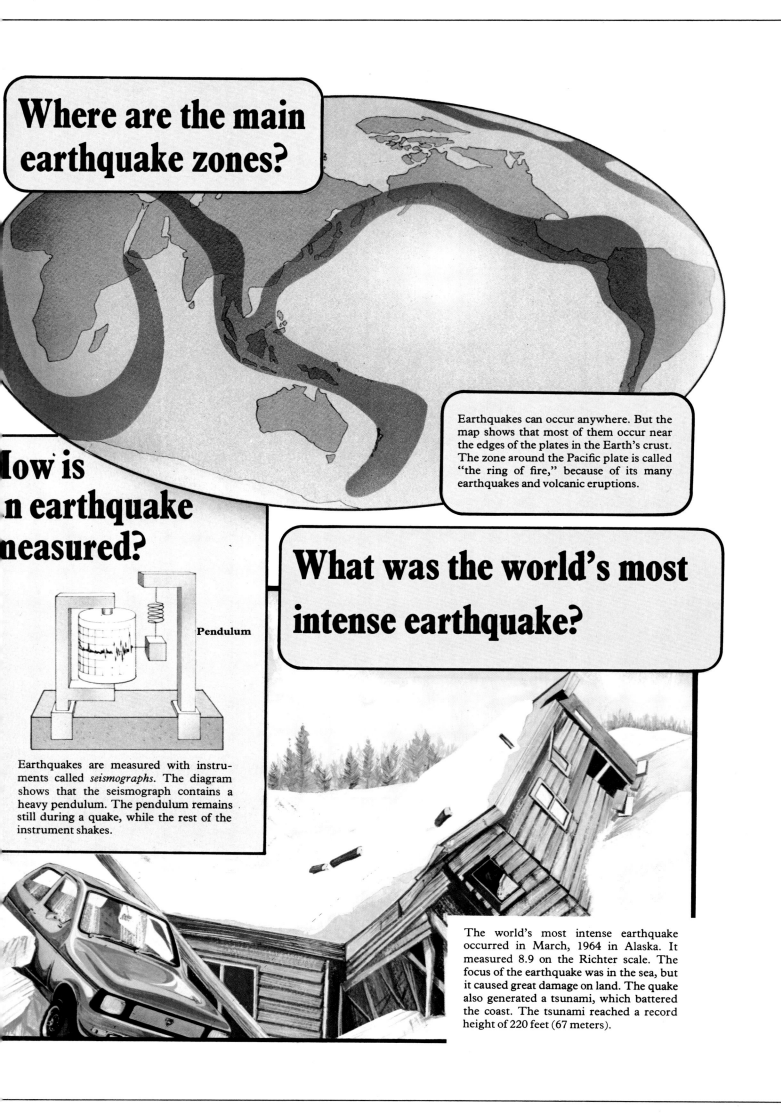

Where are the main earthquake zones?

Earthquakes can occur anywhere. But the map shows that most of them occur near the edges of the plates in the Earth's crust. The zone around the Pacific plate is called "the ring of fire," because of its many earthquakes and volcanic eruptions.

How is an earthquake measured?

Pendulum

Earthquakes are measured with instruments called *seismographs*. The diagram shows that the seismograph contains a heavy pendulum. The pendulum remains still during a quake, while the rest of the instrument shakes.

What was the world's most intense earthquake?

The world's most intense earthquake occurred in March, 1964 in Alaska. It measured 8.9 on the Richter scale. The focus of the earthquake was in the sea, but it caused great damage on land. The quake also generated a tsunami, which battered the coast. The tsunami reached a record height of 220 feet (67 meters).

ROCKS Rocks formed from molten magma are called igneous rocks. They include basalt and granite. Rocks that form from worn fragments of other rocks are called sedimentary rocks. They are so called because they mostly form as sediments in water. Sedimentary rocks include sandstones and shales. They often contain fossils, which are evidence of ancient life. Rocks that have been changed by heat, pressure, or chemical action are called metamorphic rocks.

How much sedimentary rock is there in the upper part of the Earth's crust?

How much of the Earth's land surface is covered by sedimentary rock?

Sedimentary rocks 75%

Igneous and metamorphic rocks 25%

The most common rocks exposed on the Earth's surface are sedimentary rocks. These rocks are formed mostly from worn fragments of other rocks. The sedimentary rocks mask the underlying igneous and metamorphic rocks.

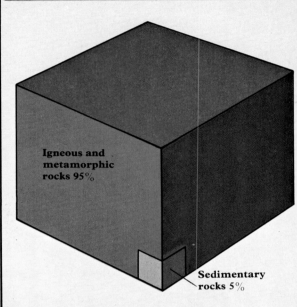

Igneous and metamorphic rocks 95%

Sedimentary rocks 5%

In the top 10 miles (16 km) of the Earth's crust, 95 per cent of the rocks are either igneous or metamorphic. Only five per cent are sedimentary. But sedimentary rocks are the commonest on the surface.

Which common rocks are igneous or metamorphic?

Basalt is an igneous rock formed from molten lava. Granite, another igneous rock, hardens underground. Heat and pressure turn shale and limestone (sedimentary rocks) into slate and marble (metamorphic rocks).

Basalt

Slate

Granite

Marble

Is coal a kind of rock?

Coal is a rock formed largely from the remains of such plants as ferns, horsetails, and mosses, which once grew in swampy forests. Most of the world's coal was formed in the Carboniferous period, between 345 and 280 million years ago.

How are fossils formed?

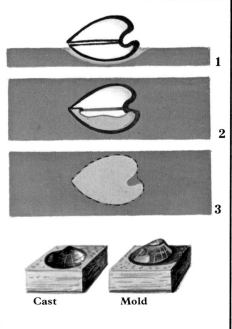

Cast   **Mold**

When a shellfish dies (1), its shell may be buried (2). Later, the shell may be dissolved away, leaving a fossil mold. Later still, the mold may be filled by a mineral, and a fossil cast is created (3).

Which are sedimentary?

Sedimentary rocks include coal and limestones, some of which formed largely from the remains of sea creatures. Other sedimentary rocks consist of such fragments as pebbles, sand, and silt. They include conglomerates, sandstones, and shale.

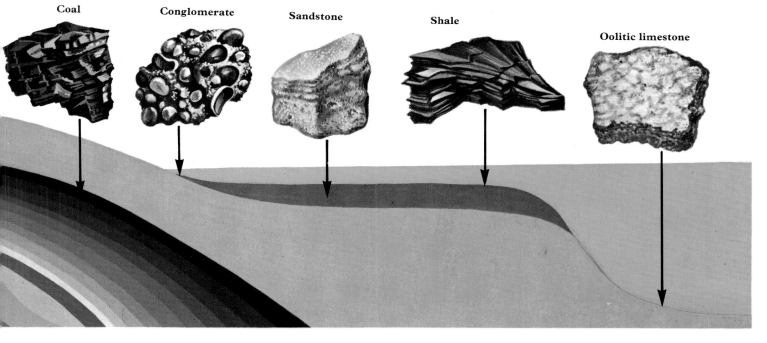

Coal   Conglomerate   Sandstone   Shale   Oolitic limestone

What does a modern coal mine look like?

RICHES FROM THE EARTH The Earth's crust is a storehouse of valuable substances, such as the fossil fuels (coal, oil, and natural gas) formed from the remains of once-living things. Many items used in everyday life are made from substances mined from the Earth. For example, steel products are made from iron and carbon, often combined with small amounts of chromium, manganese, and nickel. Mines also produce gold and precious stones. However, the Earth's resources are today being used up so quickly that we must protect and conserve them.

Modern coal mines are much safer places in which to work than those of the past. They are well ventilated by air shafts. And the miners are equipped with much labor-saving machinery to cut the coal and get it to the surface.

Pithead

Shaft

Cage

Air pump

Placing explosives

Cutting machine

Cutaway showing adjustable steel props supporting roof

Where are oil and natural gas found?

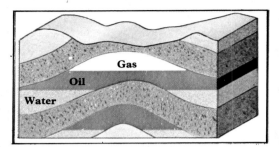

Natural gas and oil are often trapped in porous rocks (through which gases and liquids can seep) in an upfold, or *anticline*. The gas and oil cannot escape, because the porous rock is enclosed by layers of solid rock. Water often underlies the oil.

How is oil extracted from under shallow water?

Engineers build rigs in order to extract natural gas and oil from rocks beneath shallow waters, such as in the North Sea and in Lake Maracaibo, Venezuela. The rigs must be able to withstand the pounding of the waves.

What treasured substances are found in the Earth?

Valuable substances in the Earth's crust include fossil fuels and metals, some of which—for example, gold—are rare. There are also such precious stones as diamonds, rubies, and sapphires, which are cut to show off their best features and made into beautiful jewelery.

How long will Earth's reserves of fuels and metals last?

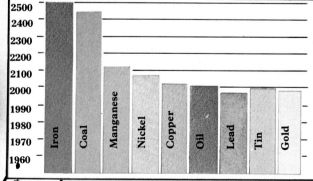

The diagram shows how long the known resources of various fuels and metals will last at present rates of consumption. The diagram does not allow for new discoveries, the re-use of existing metals, or the extraction of metals from the oceans.

Why do some places get more heat from the Sun than others?

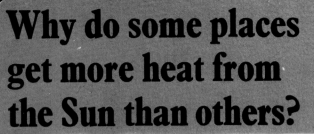

N. Pole

Sun's rays

Sun's rays

Sun's rays

S. Pole

The Sun's rays are most concentrated around the Equator. Near the poles, they spread over a much larger land area and so they are much less effective. Another factor is that, near the poles, the Sun's rays lose a lot of their heat by passing through a greater thickness of air.

CLIMATE AND WEATHER The Earth is a varied place, with many climatic regions, ranging from the icy poles to the hot equatorial lands. The climate of a region is a description of the typical or average weather. Weather is the day-to-day condition of the air. Weather features, such as temperature, air pressure, winds, rain and so on, are measured at weather stations. Weather forecasters try to predict the future weather from such information.

What instruments are used by weather forecasters?

Anemometer

Weather vane

Soil thermometer

Stevenson screen containing thermometers

Sunshine recorder

Rain gauge

At weather stations, meteorologists measure wind speeds and directions with *anemometers*, rainfall in *rain gauges*, and air temperatures with *thermometers* shaded inside a screen. They measure air pressure with *barometers* or *barographs*, and sunshine with *sunshine recorders*.

How do winds blow over the Earth?

Horse latitudes

Doldrums

Horse latitudes

The map shows the main wind systems—the polar easterlies (black arrows), the south-westerlies (white), and the trade winds (red). In general, winds blow from areas of high pressure, such as the horse latitudes and the polar regions, toward areas of low pressure, such as the doldrums.

Are there distinct climatic regions?

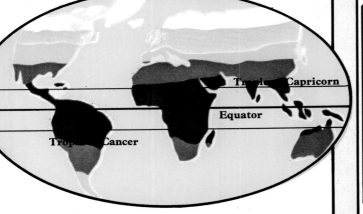

Temperature and rainfall mostly determine the five main climatic types: polar climates (white), cold forest climates (yellow), mid-latitude temperate climates (bright green), dry deserts (dark green), and tropical rainy climates (brown). In some classifications there is a mountain climate, similar to polar, but due to altitude.

What does a weather map tell us?

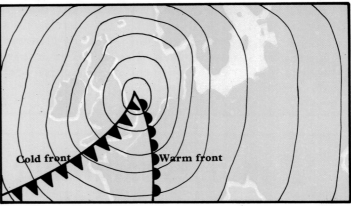

The lines on weather maps that resemble contours are *isobars*. They link places with the same atmospheric pressure. Low-pressure air systems often contain warm and cold fronts, areas associated with rain.

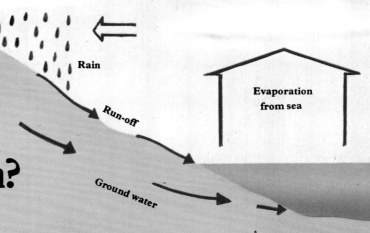

Where does the moisture in the atmosphere come from?

The water cycle brings a regular supply of fresh water to land areas. The Sun's heat evaporates water from the sea. Water vapor (a gas) rises and forms clouds. The clouds are blown over the land and the water vapor falls as rain or snow. The water then drains back into the sea.

WEATHER AND WATER MOLD THE LAND

The land is always changing. Weathering is one of the main ways in which the land is changed. It occurs, for example, when ice shatters rocks. And, in deserts, rapid changes in temperature cause rocks to peel away. Weathering also includes chemical action, such as the wearing away of limestone by rainwater. After weathering has broken up or loosened rock, other natural forces take over. In wet regions, the chief agent of erosion is running water.

Do mountains and cliffs wear away?

Rocks may be shattered by weathering. This often occurs when water fills cracks in the rocks. When the water freezes, the ice widens the cracks until, finally, the rock is split apart. The heaps of broken rock that pile up at the bottom of mountain slopes are called *scree*.

How does rainwater dissolve rock?

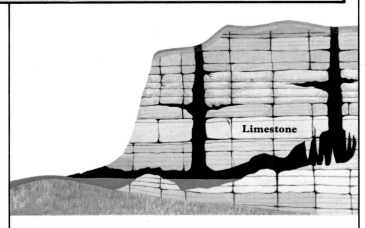

Limestone

Rainwater dissolves carbon dioxide from the air, making it a weak acid. This acid reacts with the hard rock limestone, slowly wearing it away. The water seeps through the limestone, dissolving away huge caves. The water finally reappears at a spring at the base of the limestone.

What is meant by the "water table"?

Rainwater seeps through the soil and rocks into the *zone of saturation*. There, every pore and crack in the rocks is filled with water. The top of this zone is the *water table*. Lakes and swamps occur where the water table meets the surface. Wells are drilled down to the water table.

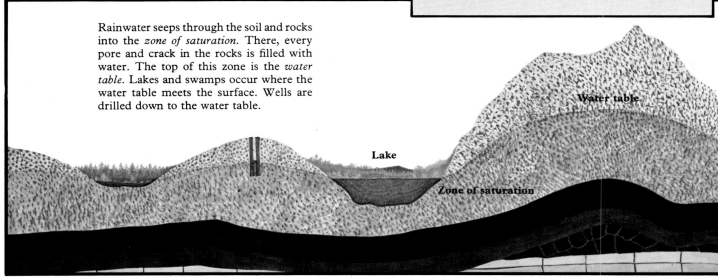

Water table

Lake

Zone of saturation

What causes springs?

Springs occur where water-bearing rock layers, called *aquifers*, reach the surface. Aquifers are often enclosed, above and below, by solid, impervious rocks, through which water cannot seep. Springs are the sources of many rivers. Other rivers flow from lakes or melting glaciers.

Spring

Aquifer

Youthful stage

Meander

Mature stage

Ox-bow lake

Old-age stage

Delta

What are the main features of a river's course?

Rivers in mountain areas are said to be *youthful*. They flow quickly and wear out deep valleys. As the slope decreases, rivers enter their vigorous *mature stage*. In *old age*, rivers flow slowly across flat plains, carrying sediment into the sea.

How are waterfalls formed?

Waterfalls usually occur at places where hard rocks resist river erosion and softer rocks, beneath the hard rock, are undercut. Occasionally, slabs of hard rock are undermined and crash down. In this way, waterfalls are always retreating.

Hard rock

Softer rock

What does a glacier look like?

Glaciers are rivers of ice that flow down valleys in mountainous regions and around the poles. Their surfaces are often littered with weathered rock. Rocks also become frozen within the ice and in its bottom and sides. This rock is called *moraine*.

THE WORK OF ICE AND WIND In cold regions, ice is a major agent of erosion. Ice sheets cover most of Antarctica and Greenland, and there are many glaciers in the mountains of temperate lands. Glacier ice forms from compacted snow. Glaciers are long tongues of ice that flow downhill. Jagged rocks, frozen in the ice, scrape over the land. In dry deserts, winds are the main force of erosion.

What effect do glaciers have on highland regions?

Horn

Arête

Cirque

U-shaped valley

Glaciers deepen valleys into a U-shape. Ice also wears out armchair-shaped hollows, called *cirques*, which are separated by knife-edged ridges, called *arêtes*.

What effect do they have on lowlands?

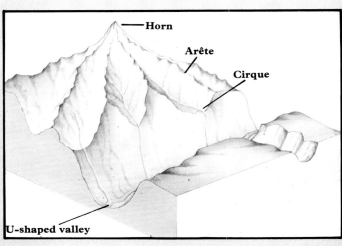

Drumlin

Terminal moraine

Ice-worn rock basin

When glaciers reach the warmer lowlands, they start to melt. Streams carry some of the moraine and spread it over the land. Other features, such as *terminal moraines*, are ridges of moraine dumped by the glacier.

What effect does the wind have on deserts?

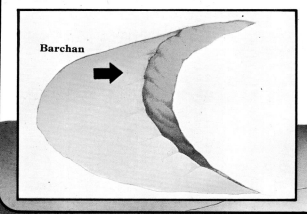

Barchan

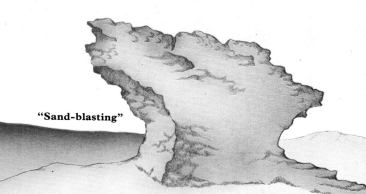

"Sand-blasting"

In dry deserts, winds blow sand into dunes, such as the crescent-shaped *barchans*. Wind-blown sand acts like a natural sand-blaster. It cuts into the lower parts of rocks, carving them into top-heavy shapes, standing on small stems—like mushrooms.

What is the largest hot desert?

The world's largest hot desert is the Sahara, in northern Africa. It was not always a desert. About 6,000 years ago, it was a grassland. But it has gradually dried up, and it is probably still spreading southward, because of severe droughts.

Sahara

What is an oasis like?

Oases are the fertile parts of deserts. They sometimes occur when underground water-bearing rocks reach the surface in hollows. Large oases support many people, who grow dates and other crops. Small oases are watering places for desert nomads.

Water-bearing rock

How high can waves in the ocean rise?

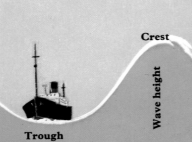

Crest

Wave height

Trough

The height of a wave is the vertical distance between the trough and the crest. The highest recorded wave was 112 feet (34 m) high. A sailor on board the USS *Ramapo* in the Pacific Ocean measured it during a gale in 1933.

THE WORK OF THE SEA The most familiar movements of the sea are waves. But waves do not move the water across the open sea. They are caused mainly by winds. When a wave passes through the sea, the water particles move around in a circle—not horizontally. Watch a corked bottle in the sea. It stays in the same place unless the wind catches it. Other movements of the sea are tides and currents. Along coasts, the sea molds the land.

What are neap tides and spring tides?

Spring tides, the highest tides, occur when the Earth, Moon, and Sun are in a straight line. The gravitational force of the Moon and Sun on ocean water is then combined. Low *neap tides* occur when the Earth, Moon, and Sun form a right angle.

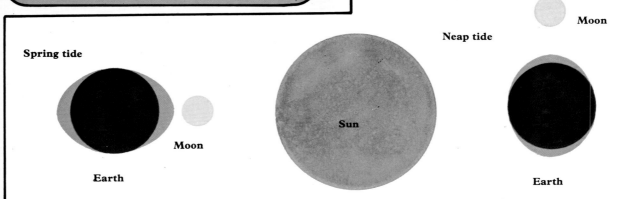

Spring tide

Earth

Moon

Sun

Neap tide

Moon

Earth

What are the main ocean currents?

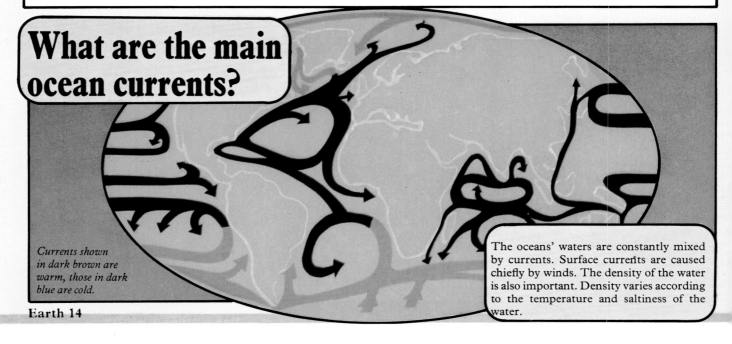

Currents shown in dark brown are warm, those in dark blue are cold.

The oceans' waters are constantly mixed by currents. Surface currents are caused chiefly by winds. The density of the water is also important. Density varies according to the temperature and saltiness of the water.

Does the sea carve away the land?

During storms, waves hurl pebbles and rocks at cliffs, creating caves (1). Caves may be worn into both sides of a headland (2). The caves may unite in a natural arch (3). When the cave collapses, a stack remains isolated in the sea (4).

Does it ever create new land?

Material worn from the land may be swept out to sea or carried along coasts by currents and waves. The material may be dumped in long ridges, called *spits*. Sometimes, it forms a bar across a bay, sealing off the bay from the sea.

A-Z of the Earth

A

abyss The name for the deep parts of the ocean beyond the continental slope.

air *See* ATMOSPHERE.

Alps A high, fold-mountain range in south-central Europe. The highest peak is Mont Blanc, in France. It is 15,781 feet (4,810 m) above sea level.

Amazon River Mainly in Brazil, South America, it is the world's second longest river, about 4,000 miles (6,440 km) long.

anemometer An instrument used at weather stations to measure the speed, and often the direction, of the wind.

anticline An up-fold or arch of rock layers caused by pressure.

arête A knife-edged ridge between two armchair-shaped depressions called *cirques*. Arêtes are formed by ice action in mountain regions.

artesian well A kind of well in which the underground water-bearing rock is tilted. The trapped water is under pressure and it gushes to the surface.

atmosphere The mixture of gases that surrounds the Earth—mainly oxygen (20.95%), nitrogen (78.09%), and argon (0.93%). Tiny amounts of various other gases also occur. It also contains water vapor and dust. The atmosphere becomes thinner the higher you travel.

avalanche A mass of snow and ice, often containing much rock, which crashes down mountainsides. They may be started by thaws or by sudden, loud sounds.

axis An imaginary line joining the North Pole, the center of the Earth, and the South Pole. The Earth rotates on its axis once every 24 hours.

B

bar A ridge of sand and shingle that runs parallel to the coast or from a headland across a bay or estuary.

barchan A crescent-shaped sand dune.

barometer Any instrument used to measure air pressure. One kind consists of a sealed glass tube containing mercury, which is suspended upside-down in a bath of mercury. As the air pressure increases, it pushes down on the mercury, and the mercury in the tube rises.

basalt An igneous rock, formed when burning-hot lava cools and solidifies.

batholiths Enormous dome-shaped masses of igneous rock. They are formed underground when molten magma hardens.

block mountains Mountains formed when a large block of land is pushed upward between faults (cracks) in the Earth's crust.

boulder clay The name for material dumped on the land by glaciers. It contains rocks embedded in extremely fine, ground-down sand and clay.

C

canyon A river-worn valley that has extremely steep sides.

Carlsbad Caverns A cave system in New Mexico. They contain the world's largest cave. It is called the Big Room, and is about 4,000 feet (1,220 m) long, nearly 328 feet (100 m) high, and about 656 feet (200 m) wide.

cave A hollow beneath the Earth's surface. Some caves occur in cliffs on the coast or in hardened lava. But most occur in limestone rocks, which are dissolved away by water containing carbon dioxide.

chalk A white or greyish limestone. Many kinds of chalk consist largely of the remains of once-living organisms. Note that blackboard "chalk" consists of a quite different material, gypsum.

cirques Armchair-shaped depressions in mountain regions. These steep-sided, round hollows often contain lakes, called *tarns*, which were worn out by ice.

climate The average, or typical, weather of a place or region.

cloud A mass of water droplets or ice crystals in the air. There are two main kinds of clouds. Some, such as *stratus*, form in layers or sheets. Others, such as *cumulus*, form in huge heaps.

coal A rock formed from the remains of decayed plants.

conglomerate A sedimentary rock containing rounded pebbles embedded in finer material. This rock formed at the mouths of rivers, where the heavy pebbles were dropped in the shallow water, while fine silt and mud were swept out to sea.

continent The name for large land-masses and the islands that lie around them. They are as follows:

Asia	16,988,000 sq mi
Africa	11,506,000 sq mi
North America	9,390,000 sq mi
South America	6,795,000 sq mi
Antarctica	5,500,000 sq mi
Europe	3,745,000 sq mi
Oceania (including Australia)	2,968,000 sq mi

continental drift The name for the movement of continents around the face of the Earth. According to the theory of continental drift, all the continents were once joined together, but they split apart and drifted to their present positions in the last 200 million years.

continental shelf The shallow sea bed around continents. It ends where the continental slope begins. The edge of the continental shelf is the true edge of the continents.

continental slope The steep slope joining the continental shelf to the abyss.

convection currents The type of current that occurs when a flame is placed under a pan of water. Particles of water expand and rise. At the surface, they spread sideways, cool, and finally sink to the bottom. Similar currents occur in the air. For example, at the Equator, warm air rises and spreads north and south, finally sinking again in the horse latitudes. Convection currents also occur in the rocks of the Earth's mantle, under the crust, where the spreading of the rock under the crust causes continental drift.

core The Earth's core has a diameter of 4,300 miles (6,920 km). The inner core is solid, but the outer core consists of molten, liquid rock.

crevasse A deep crack in a glacier or ice sheet.

crust The Earth's crust is a thin shell about 4 miles (6 km) thick under the oceans and up to 37–43 miles (60–70 km) thick under continental mountain ranges.

currents, ocean Ocean water is moved by currents. Winds cause most surface ocean currents, but some are caused by differences in density, resulting from differing temperatures of differing amounts of salt in the water.

D

day The time taken by the Earth to revolve once on its axis.

Dead Sea An extremely salty lake between Israel and Jordan. Its shore is the world's lowest place on land—1,289 feet (393 m) below sea level.

delta An area of land formed at the mouth of a river from sediments dropped there by the river.

desert A dry area, usually with an average of less than 10 inches (250 mm) of rain per year.

dinosaur The name for a large group of animals that lived in the Mesozoic era between about 225 and 65 million years ago. Our knowledge of them comes from fossils, and no one knows for sure why they died out.

doldrums The zone around the Equator in which the trade winds blow. The zone is marked by calm weather.

drumlin An egg-shaped hill formed from boulder clay deposited by ice.

dune A mound or ridge of sand.

E

earthquakes Sudden movements of the land along faults. Earthquake tremors may cause great damage.

Equator An imaginary line around the Earth, half-way between the North and South Poles.

equinoxes Two days every year when the Sun is directly overhead at the Equator. The *spring equinox* occurs on about March 21 and the *autumnal equinox* on about September 23. Equinox means "equal night." At the equinoxes, everywhere on Earth has a 12-hour day and night.

erosion The wearing away of the land by weathering, running water, ice, sea waves, and winds.

esker A ridge of ice-worn material formed by a stream that once flowed under an ice sheet or glacier.

estuary The part of the mouth of a river that is affected by tides.

Everest Mountain on the Nepal–Tibet border in the Himalayas. The world's highest peak, it is 29,028 feet (8,848 m) above sea level.

F

fault A break or crack in rocks, along which the rocks have moved.

fiord or **fjord** A deep, U-shaped valley worn out by a glacier, but now filled by the sea.

flood plain A flat area that is often flooded when an old-age river overflows its banks.

fold mountains Formed by lateral (sideways) pressure, which pushes rocks upwards in great loops or folds.

fossils Evidence in rocks of once-living animals and plants.

G

glaciation The action of ice on the land. The ice molds the rocks, producing distinctive landforms.

glacier A mass of ice that moves downward from its source in a mountain area along a valley.

Grand Canyon A deep valley worn out by the Colorado River in the southwestern United States. It is about 200 miles (320 km) long, up to 1 mile (1·6 km) deep, and 2 to 18 miles (3 to 29 km) wide.

granite A common igneous rock, formed when magma solidifies underground.

Greenwich Mean Time The standard time at the Greenwich Observatory, London, which lies on longitude 0°. Time zones are measured east and west of Greenwich.

ground water Water that seeps through the soil and the rocks that lie beneath the Earth's surface.

H

Hawaiian volcanoes These do not erupt explosively, but emit streams of molten lava, which flow great distances. Because they do not explode, they are said to be "quiet" volcanoes. Hawaiian volcanoes resemble upturned saucers.

Himalayas The world's highest mountain range. These fold mountains include Everest, the world's highest peak.

horn A pointed mountain peak, worn away by glaciation.

horse latitudes Areas of high air pressure around 30° North and 30° South. Trade winds and westerlies blow outward from the horse latitudes.

horst A block of land raised up as a ridge between faults.

I-K

iceberg A floating mass of ice that has broken away from an ice sheet or glacier. Only about nine-tenths of an iceberg appears above the waves.

igneous rocks Rocks formed when molten magma solidifies either on the surface or underground.

International Date Line A line around 180° longitude, on the opposite side of the Earth to the prime meridian (0° longitude). East of the prime meridian, 180° represents a *gain* of 12 hours. West of the prime meridian, 180° represents a *loss* of 12 hours. Hence the time difference on either side of the International Date Line is 24 hours, or 1 day.

Krakatoa A volcanic island between Java and Sumatra that exploded in 1883. It was the biggest explosion of modern times.

L

landslides Movements of rock and soil down steep slopes. They may be caused by heavy rain or by earthquakes.

latitude Lines drawn on maps parallel to the equator (0° latitude) are called *lines of latitude* or *parallels*. Other lines, at right-angles to lines of latitude and passing through both poles, are called *lines of longitude*.

lava Molten rock, or magma, which appears on the Earth's surface. .

limestone A common sedimentary rock, formed mostly of calcium carbonate. Chalk is the purest form.

longitude *See* LATITUDE.

M

magma Molten rock that may erupt as lava or harden underground.

magnetic poles The Earth is like a giant magnet. Like all magnets, it has two magnetic poles. These lie near the geographical poles.

mantle The section of the Earth between the thin crust and the core.

marble A metamorphic rock formed when great heat and pressure *metamorphose* (change) limestone.

Mauna Kea A Hawaiian volcano, the world's highest mountain measured from the sea bed. It has a height of 33,474 feet (10,203 m), but only 13,796 feet (4,205 m) is above sea level.

meander A bend in a river.

meridian A line of longitude.

metamorphic rocks Rocks that have been *metamorphosed*, changed by heat, pressure, or chemical action.

moraine Rocks and clay deposited by ice sheets and glaciers.

mountains They may be volcanic or formed by lateral pressure (fold mountains) or by the raising up of land between faults (horsts and block mountains).

N

nappe A fold in rocks that has been sheared and pushed forwards, masking the rocks beneath it.

natural gas Probably formed from the remains of once-living organisms. It is found trapped in porous rocks, often above deposits of petroleum (oil).

Nile The world's longest river. It flows 4,415 miles (6,670 km) through north-eastern Africa.

nuée ardente A feature of some volcanic eruptions. The term means "glowing cloud" and, when the volcano explodes, it emits a cloud of hot gases, steam, and fragments of ash which rolls downhill, burning all in its path.

O

oasis A place in a desert where there is surface water. It may be a small pond or a large area, such as the Nile valley in Egypt.

Old Faithful The name of a geyser in Yellowstone National Park. On the average, it erupts a jet of hot water and steam once every 65 minutes.

ox-bow lake Some rivers straighten their courses by cutting through the necks of meanders (bends). The former meander is then cut off and remains, for a while, as an ox-bow lake.

P

Pangaea The name for an ancient continent that, about 200 million years ago, consisted of all of our present continents joined together. But Pangaea split up and the parts moved to their present positions because of continental drift.

parallel A line of latitude.

Pelée, Mount A volcano on Martinique, a West Indian island. It erupted in 1902 and a huge *nuée ardente* (glowing cloud) destroyed the town of St. Pierre.

plateau The name for a mostly level upland region.

poles The points at the end of the Earth's axis—the North Pole and the South Pole. The magnetic poles are near the geographical poles.

Pompeii A former Roman town near the Bay of Naples, Italy. In AD 79, the nearby volcano, Mt. Vesuvius, exploded. A cloud of hot pumice and ash rained down on Pompeii, which remained buried and forgotten for hundreds of years.

prime meridian The name for 0° longitude, which passes from the North Pole, through Greenwich Observatory, London, to the South Pole. The line was fixed by international agreement in 1884.

R

rain gauge An instrument used at weather stations to measure precipitation (rain, snow, hail, and so on).

rift valley A valley formed when a block of land sinks down between faults. They are often deep and steep-sided, and contain many lakes.

S

Sahara In northern Africa, it is the world's largest hot desert. It covers about 3 million square miles (7.8 million square kilometers).

San Francisco earthquake Occurred in 1906 when there was a sudden shift along the nearby San Andreas fault. Fires caused by broken gas pipes and electrical short circuits destroyed much of San Francisco. Scientists are now predicting another earthquake in the area.

Santorini (or **Thera**) A Greek island where, in about 1470 BC, the world's greatest volcanic explosion occured. A *tsunami* (ocean wave) triggered by the explosion may have destroyed the ancient Minoan civilization in the eastern Mediterranean.

scree Broken, weathered rock that piles up at the foot of mountain slopes.

seasons The seasons occur because the Earth's axis is tilted. As a result, as the Earth orbits the Sun, the Northern and Southern Hemispheres are tilted toward and away from the Sun.

sedimentary rocks Formed from eroded rock fragments; or from the remains of once-living organisms; or from chemicals precipitated from water.

seismograph An instrument used to record and measure the intensity of earthquakes.

sink hole A pit in a limestone outcrop. It was dissolved out by rain water and it leads down to the caves below.

slate A hard metamorphic rock formed when soft shale is subjected to pressure and heat.

solar system The name for all the bodies, including the Earth, that orbit around the Sun.

solstices Two days every year when the overhead Sun reaches its northernmost and southernmost points. The summer solstice, with the Sun overhead at the Tropic of Cancer, is on about June 21. The winter solstice, when the Sun is overhead at the southern Tropic of Capricorn, occurs on about December 21.

spit A ridge of worn material deposited by waves and currents in the sea.

spring A flow of ground water on to the surface, where it may form a stream.

stack An isolated pillar of rock in the sea, which was cut off from the land by wave action.

stalactite A long, icicle-like growth of rock from the roof of a limestone cave. It is formed from calcite precipitated from dripping water.

stalagmite A pillar of rock that grows upward from the floor of a limestone cave.

sunshine recorder An instrument used to measure the number of hours of sunshine that occur each day.

T

thermometer An instrument for measuring temperatures.

tides The twice-daily rise and fall of sea level. They are caused by the gravitational pull of the Moon and Sun on the Earth's ocean waters.

time zone A region that has the same standard time. The world is split up into time zones, based mainly on longitude.

trade winds Winds that blow toward the Equator from the horse latitudes. In the Northern Hemisphere, they blow from the north-east to the south-west. In the Southern Hemisphere, they blow from the south-east to the north-west.

tsunami A destructive ocean wave caused by earthquakes or volcanic explosions. In the open sea, they are low but fast-moving waves. As they near land, the water piles up. The record height of a tsunami is 220 feet (67 m).

UV

U-shaped valley A steep-sided, flat-bottomed valley worn out by a glacier.

Vesuvius A volcano in southern Italy, which erupted explosively in AD 79 and buried the town of Pompeii. Most eruptions since AD 79, including the last in 1944, have been accompanied by lava flows.

W

water cycle The way in which water constantly circulates from the oceans to the land and back again.

waterfall A vertical fall of water in a river's course.

water table A surface, underground, below which the rocks are saturated with water.

weather The day-to-day condition of the air, including its temperature, the amount of moisture in it, and so on.

weathering The wearing away of rocks by the action of weather, such as the freezing of water, which splits rocks open, or the dissolving action of rain water (a weak acid) on some rocks.

weather vanes Used to measure wind directions.

well A hole dug down to the water table to obtain water.

westerlies Winds that blow polewards from the horse latitudes. In the Northern Hemisphere, they are called the south-westerlies. In the Southern Hemisphere, they are the north-westerlies.

winds Movements of air masses.

Y

year The time taken by the Earth to orbit the Sun—365 days, 5 hours, 48 minutes, and 46 seconds. Calendar years have 365 days, but we have leap years to make up for the extra time.